STUDY GUIDE

ABNORMAL PSYCHOLOGY

AN EXPERIMENTAL CLINICAL APPROACH

FOURTH EDITION

DAVISON/NEALE

PREPARED BY

DOUGLAS HINDMAN

JOHN WILEY & SONS

New York Chichester Brisbane Toronto Singapore

ISBN 0 471 82775 4

Printed in the United States of America

10 9 8 7 6 5

To The Student

This study guide accompanies *Abnormal Psychology: An Experimental Clinical Approach, 4th Edition* by Davison and Neale. It is based on the experiences and criticisms of hundreds of students who used earlier versions of it in my classes.

Each chapter includes a number of sections to help you study the text. The *Overview* section places the text chapter in context showing how it relates to the chapters that preceed and follow it. The *Chapter Summary* and *Study Objectives* identify the primary topics covered in the chapter. The *Key Terms* allows you room to write in the definitions of new, technical terms, introduced in the chapter. The *Study Questions* guide you to the main concepts of each section and provide room for you to write in answers. Lastly the *Self-test* provides multiple-choice and short answer items so you can check your knowledge.

Study guides can be effective aids to studying. To help you further, this guide includes introductory sections on how to study and on identifying and correcting any study problems you may have. Many of my students have found these sections useful.

Abnormal psychology is a fascinating, but complex, topic for many students. Hopefully this guide will make your study of it easier and more satisfying. Your comments and suggestions for improving this guide would be most welcome.

CONTENTS

STUDYING IN THIS COURSE (AND IN OTHER COURSES, TOO)

This study guide is designed, in part, to help you develop good study skills. If you typically get good grades, you probably already have good study skills and will find little difficulty adapting them to this course. On the other hand, if you often get poor grades, you may have poor study skills. This guide is designed to help students with poor study habits develop better ones and to help even successful students learn to study more efficiently. If you will spend a little time consciously working on your study skills, you can help the process along.

We're convinced (though it might be hard to prove) that few college students make poor grades because they are "dumb". If you find yourself spending more time studying than others—and getting poorer grades—it is likely you aren't using your time efficiently. Of course, if you don't put much time into studying, the reason for your low grades is obvious. The traditional rule of thumb for undergraduates is that you should spend two hours outside of class for every hour in class. For a normal undergraduate course load, that works out to about a forty-hour work week.

If you do put enough time into your studying, how should you spend that time? As you begin to study a new chapter, follow this system:

1. Survey the entire chapter briefly. Take abut five minutes to look over the titles and headings, read the introduction and summary, and get a general idea of the material. Ask yourself what you will be studying. Figure out how the text is organized to cover the topic. Don't read the chapter in detail yet. This brief initial survey will help you focus your attention, familiarize you with new vocabulary and concepts, and help you retain more information than even several rereadings of the chapter.

2. Look over the first portion of the chapter and turn the main heading or topic into a question. What are you being told? This study guide will help you formulate such questions.

3. Read the first portion, actively looking for the answer to your question. It is important that you actively seek the answer as you read.

4. Write down the answer in your guide, striving to use as few words as possible. Being concise is important. When you can condense a long portion into a few words that express the key idea, you know you understand the idea clearly. Also, the few words you write down will be meaningful to you so you will remember them. Don't worry about writing complete sentences or elaborating excessively. The fewer words you can use, the better you probably understand and will remember the concept.

   Repeat Steps 3 and 4 until you finish the chapter.

5. Recite after you finish the chapter. Go back and quiz yourself. Do this aloud. Actively speaking and listening to yourself will help you remember. Look at each question and try to repeat the answer without looking. Cover your answers with a sheet of paper so you don't unconsciously peek. Put several questions together and try to recite all the answers to a whole general topic. Get with a classmate to quiz each other, or ask a friend to read the questions and tell you if your answers make sense. If you've done the earlier steps well, this won't take much time.

6. Review. After you finish your first study of a chapter, set aside a few minutes every week to review the material. Spend 10 or 15 minutes reciting the material as in Step 5. If you review regularly, you'll find it takes little time to refresh yourself for an exam.

This technique is one variation of a study method called "SQ4R" (Survey, Question, Read, Rite, Recite, Review). If you're not used to it, it may seem a bit complicated at first. If you check around, though, you will find that the "good" students are already using it or a similar system. Research suggests that SQ4R works. You may find that it takes a bit of extra effort to get used to, but remember that studying is a skill and that learning any skill (like typing, driving, and playing ball) takes some time and practice. You will find, though, that your efforts to improve your study will pay off in this and in your other courses.

If you need more help, many schools have a learning lab or learning skills center where you can get individualized help. Ask your instructor what facilities your school provides. The next section of this guide also provides help for particular study problems.

A STUDENT'S DIAGNOSTIC GUIDE TO STUDY PROBLEMS

Developing effective study skills is a continuing process. This guide evolved from many years experience in helping students with study problems. Even if you're not having problems, you may still find it helpful to review your study habits and look for ways to improve them. Although written for this study guide, the ideas presented should also apply to the study procedures you use in other courses.

To begin checking your study habits, look over a filled-in section of your study guide. (In another class, look over your study notes.) Analyze your answers (or notes) to see which of the following descriptions apply. Are your answers:

A. Concise? In your own words? Do they express the central idea clearly? This is ideal. Students who consistenly write brief, accurate answers rarely have trouble on quizzes. If you are missing too many items on quizzes, you probably need to review more. You will find some suggestions in the material on SQ4R in the previous section of this guide.

B. Verbose? This is common. If your answers are long but still clear and in your own words, your problem is not too serious—but it's still time consuming to write, and difficult to review and remember all that verbiage.

C. Quotes from the text? The danger in extensive quoting is that you copy words out of the text without really understanding them. Then you try to memorize the words. Memorizing is difficult and, since you didn't understand the basic idea, you'll get caught whenever the question is worded a little differently on a quiz. Often students write long quotations in their study guides because they are used to underlining in other courses and are trying to transfer the technique to a study guide. Underlining in textbooks can be dangerous for the same reason. While an occasional important phrase may be useful to quote, a long passage is rarely worth quoting.

D. Confused and muddled? (Ask someone else's opinion.) Often when you're writing a confused, meaningless statement, you'll realize it's meaningless before you even finish it. If you start to write something in your guide and realize it's meaningless—stop! Restudy the text or get help. If your answer doesn't make sense to you, it won't to your instructor. Sometimes, long, verbose answers are also muddled because you lost your train of thought in the middle of writing.

E. Wrong? Answers that you simply took from the text incorrectly are hard to correct if you didn't realize your error at the time. Sometimes incorrect answers occur when you see what looks like the answer at the start of a section of text and write it down without reading the rest of the section. Students who read slowly or have comprehension difficulties frequently misinterpret the text in this way. If you discover that you frequently get the wrong answer in your study guide without realizing it, you should check with your instructor. Your instructor may be able to suggest some techniques or campus services to help you improve your reading skills.

Now that you have some ideas about what you're doing (or not doing) as you study, you may want to consider changing some of your study habits. Here are some suggestions:

A. Key words. In filling out your study guide, use as few words as possible. Try to find the few key words that summarize the idea and will help you recall it on the quiz. (You shouldn't oversimplify, of course, but this is not a problem for most students.) Don't write complete sentences; instead, "telegraph" the idea. Play a game with yourself to use the fewest words possible. There are a number of advantages to being brief in this way.

1. You will force yourself to know the material thoroughly. You can't reduce a large section of text to a few words without understanding the idea of that section clearly. This is why you should avoid using someone else's study guide or underlined text. The learning value is not in having the important words identified but in the process of discovering for yourself which words are important.

2. When you review the unit, you won't have to wade through a lot of extraneous words to get to the idea. Your notes will be brief and meaningful.

3. On the quiz, you'll need only to remember your key words in order to recall the entire concept. Since you know the concept, not merely the memorized words, you will be better prepared to answer questions that ask you to illustrate, apply, or compare concepts.

B. Reading speed. Slow reading can lead to a number of problems:

- It takes too long to get through the material.
- You lose interest before you get to the main point.
- You forget the first part of an idea before you get to the end. (You "lose the forest for the trees.")

Slow readers often:

- Fail to get the important point.
- Cannot understand a concept if it is never clearly stated in one sentence.
- Give long memorized answers they can't explain.
- Misinterpret material. (You take so long getting through a sentence that you start reading in your own ideas.)

If the description above reminds you of yourself, you might want to check your reading speed. To check your speed, have someone time you while you read for exactly five minutes. Estimate the number of words you read and divide by five.

To estimate the number of words you read, count the number of words in the five lines and divide by five to get the average numbeer of words per line. Then count the number of lines read and multiply by the number of words per line.

For textbook material, an efficient reading speed is about 350 to 400 words per minute—depending on the difficulty of the topic and your familiarity with it. For novels and other leisure reading, many students can read 600 to 800 words per minute and "speed readers" can read much faster. Remember that understanding and flexibility in your reading style is more important than speed, but often a slight increase in speed can actually help improve your understanding.

You can increase your reading speed to some extent by conscious effort. If you watch someone read, you'll notice that their eyes move in "jerks" across the line. Our eyes can read words only when stopped; we read a group of words, then move our eyes, read the next group of words, and so on. To increase reading speed, then, try to take in more words with each eye stop. Don't be concerned with every "and" or "but." Do try to notice the main words that carry the meaning. Read for ideas, not words.

If you read very slowly, you should consider seeking special help. Most campuses now have reading laboratories where you can get specialized instruction and help in increasing your reading speed. Ask your instructor if your school offers such help.

C. Underlining in the text. Many people underline or highlight their texts and it works well—sometimes. For most people underlining is not as efficient as taking notes or using a study guide emphasizing key words. The danger in underlining is that students tend to underline things to be learned later rather than learning them now. They may end up with half the words in the chapter underlined and none of them learned. If you must underline, try to underline as few words as possible in the same way as suggested for taking notes under "Key words" above. Avoid used textbooks that someone else underlined. Not only may they have been a poor underliner, but the value of underlining (like the value of taking notes) is in doing it yourself and in learning what's important in the process.

D. Reading the text. Some students think that effective study means to "read the chapter" three or four times. This is tremendously inefficient! Without the discipline of note-taking (or underlining), there is a strong tendency to skip over difficult material and generally to "tune out." People who reread the material several times often have the experience of suddenly realizing that they've just been looking at the words and can't remember a thing they've read. Moreover, research indicates that when people reread the material, they tend to skip over the same portions they didn't understand the first time.

If you find yourself caught in the habit of reading chapters over and over, break the habit! Use an efficient system like the SQ4R (described earlier) or a similar study system to invest your time wisely. SQ4R has been shown to boost learning by 40 to 60 percent over traditional reading habits.

1 Introduction Historical and Scientific Considerations

OVERVIEW

The first five chapters cover basic ideas and issues in abnormal psychology. These chapters are a background for the rest of the text which covers forms of psychopathology and related topics.

The first two chapters discuss viewpoints on the nature of psychopathology. Psychologists, as well as the general public, still disagree on exactly how to view people with psychological problems. For example, should these people be viewed as "sick," as having "adjustment problems," or as the victims of faulty socialization or learning?

The way we view these problems becomes especially important when discussing ways of classifying and studying psychopathology - in Chapters 3, 4, and 5. For example, if we view people with these problems as being "mentally ill", then we would want to diagnose what illness the person has and develop ways to study and treat the illness. If we perceive these people instead as having trouble adjusting to society or as having learned ineffective ways of getting along in the world, then we might want to categorize and study their problems somewhat differently.

CHAPTER SUMMARY

Chapter one covers three major topics. The Mental Health Professions briefly describes the training, skills, and orientations of the various mental health professions.

The History of Psychopathology shows that different historical periods have emphasized one of three views concerning the causes of psychopathology: Demonology (caused by evil spirits), Somatogenesis (bodily causes) or Psychogenesis (psychological or mental causes). These three views have led society to study and treat disturbed individuals in different ways.

Science: A Human Enterprise points out that science is both objective (in gathering data) and subjective (reflecting the views of the people who gather the data). That is, the paradigms or theories of scientists influence the kinds of data they seek and the way they make sense out of what they find. Paradigms can also make it difficult for scientists to recognize phenomena that don't fit the paradigm. Hypnosis is discussed both as a historical topic and as an illustration of the influence of paradigms.

STUDY OBJECTIVES

After studying Chapter 1 you should know

1. That the text takes a scientific rather than a phenomenological approach to understanding abnormal behavior.

2. The different types of professionals involved in the field of mental health and that their orientations typically reflect their school of training not their degree.

3. There have been differing views on the cause of abnormal behavior throughout history although contemporary thoughts basically stem from the somatogenic and the psychogenic viewpoints, which emerged 2,000 years ago and in the 18th century, respectively.

4. That the way in which the causes of abnormal behavior are perceived deeply affects the way in which abnormal behavior is treated (e.g. trephining).

5. That abnormal behavior has been treated differently and often inhumanely in the past, although not as poorly as often portrayed nor are current practices as enlightened as sometimes depicted.

6. That although the scientific enterprise strives to be objective, there are intruding elements of subjectivity, such as assuming what type of method to use to collect data or what type of questions to ask (paradigms).

KEY TERMS

Psychiatrist (p. 6) M.D. degree - postgraduate training

Psychoanalyst (p. 6) trained at psychoanalytic institute usually private practice

Clinical psychologist (p. 6) usually Ph.D.

Psychiatric social worker (p. 7) Master of social work degree

Counseling psychologist (p. 7) less emphasis on research (sim. to clinical psych)

Paraprofessional (p. 7) no advanced degrees; conduct therapy under professionals

Psychopathologist (p. 7) research on how abn. behavior develops

Demonology (p. 7)

cathartic method: reliving of earlier emotional catastrophe & tension produced by previously forgotten thoughts about the event

Somatogenesis (p. 8) bodily disfunctions disturb behavior

Hippocrates (p. 8) mental illness had natural causes
mania, melancholia, phrenitis

Zeitgeist (p. 8) intellectual / emotional orientation at time of Hippo.

Malleus Maleficarum (p. 10)
(legal & theological acc.) guide witch hunts

Moral treatment (p. 15)
treatment as sick humans

Philippe Pinel (p. 15) La Bicêtre

Emil Kraepelin (p. 18) dementia praecox (schizophrenia)
symptoms manic - depression

General paresis (p. 18) each mental illness was distinct from others
disease

Psychogenesis (p. 19)
psychic malfunctions

Anton Mesmer (p. 20) early practitioners of hypnosis

Hypnosis (p. 20)

Jean Charcot (p. 20) neurologist - studied hysterical states

Josef Breuer (p. 21) cathartic method

Paradigms (p. 23) set of assumptions that outline science inquiry

specify what problems will be investigated & how they will go about investigating

STUDY QUESTIONS

THE MENTAL HEALTH PROFESSIONS (p. 6 - 7)

1. Distinguish among psychiatrists, psychoanalysts, and clinical psychologists in terms of their basic training and their typical treatment techniques. (p. 6 - 7)

HISTORY OF PSYCHOPATHOLOGY (p. 7 - 22)

2. Which was the earliest theory of deviant behavior? How did it explain abnormality and what kinds of treatment resulted from it? (p. 7)

3. What theory of deviant behavior emerged under Hippocrates? According to this theory, what was the cause of deviance and how did treatment emphases change as a result? (p. 8)

Somatogenic

bodily disorders disrupt thought & action

Treatment:

natural remedies (tranquility, sobriety, abstinence from sex) - Hippocrates

4. What is the present conventional view regarding those people labeled as witches during the dark ages? What alternative does the text propose? (p. 8 - 13)

5. As the Inquisition ended, what new method of dealing with the mentally ill emerged? What conditions and treatment methods developed? (p. 13 - 17)

6. Describe how contemporary views of somatogenesis and psychogenesis emerged. Describe an early success of each view. (p. 18 - 22)

SCIENCE: A HUMAN ENTERPRISE (p. 22 - 26)

7. By pointing out that science is a human enterprise, the text emphasizes that science is both objective and subjective. In what way is it (a) objective and (b) subjective? (p. 22)

8. What is a paradigm? Why are paradigms (a) necessary and (b) potentially limiting? (p. 22 - 23)

Paradigms: what problems will be investigated & how they will go about investigating

(A) provide basic rules of research

(B) inevitable biases, affect interpretation

9. Describe the work of Langer and Abelson (1974) as an example of paradigms in abnormal psychology. How does their study illustrate the role of paradigms? (p. 23 - 26)

SELF-TEST, CHAPTER 1

MULTIPLE-CHOICE

1. One problem in studying abnormal psychology is our closeness to the subject matter of behavior. As a result
   A. The field is very ambiguous
   B. We must rely on paradigms to study abnormality
   C. We have pre-conceived ideas that are hard to set aside
   D. Psychology can never be truly scientific

2. An individual with a M. D. plus special training in working with individuals with psychological problems would be called a:
   A. Psychiatrist
   B. Clinical psychologist
   C. Psychoanalyst
   D. Psychopathologist

3. Among the changes during the dark ages which led to the inquisition were:
   A. Belief in the power of the devil
   B. Increased use of systematic observation
   C. Lack of other social problems to focus peoples' interest
   D. Growth of large mental hospitals.

4. Which of the following led to the early development of asylums for the insane?
   A. Discovery of the cause of syphilis
   B. Desire to get rid of socially undesirable people
   C. Development of the psychogenic model
   D. Need to protect people from the inquisition

5. Which of the following comes closest to the views of Philippe Pinel who removed the chains from French asylum patients?

A. Demonology
B. Somatogenesis
C. Psychogenesis psychological or mental
D. Malleus maleficarum

6. The discovery of the nature and cause of syphilis was historically important because

A. It helped scientists appreciate the need to use many paradigms simultaneously
B. Large asylums were no longer needed
C. It attracted many new professionals into the field of treatment
D. It showed the somatogenic theory could be effective

7. Followers of the psychogenic paradigm would be most likely to use treatments such as;

A. Trephining
B. Bleeding
C. Tranquilizers
D. Hypnotism

8. Paradigms are necessary in order for science to:

A. Evaluate facts objectively
B. Insure that all possible data is considered
C. Define the methods of investigation to use
D. Remain sensitive to the suffering experienced by the mentally ill

9. In Langer and Abelson's study, used to illustrate the influence of paradigms in abnormal psychology,

A. Psychologists used a variety of paradigms to cure the same problem
B. People developed psychotic symptoms after eating ergot tainted grain
C. Clinicians were asked to rate a man described as either a job applicant or a mental patient
D. Historical records showed that moral treatment was as effective as psychotherapy

10. If you are told that scientist, Dr. X, uses paradigms in his research you should
   A. Be impressed since this shows Dr. X is doing sophisticated work
   B. Wonder if Dr. X is doing worthwhile research
   C. Realize that his work is quite unusual
   D. Not care since all researchers use paradigms

SHORT ANSWER

1. Students of abnormal psychology need to have great ____________ because human behavior is not well understood.

2. A ____________ has advanced training in scientific research and in using both scientific and applied methods to work with disturbed individuals.

3. Define "demonology".

4. Hippocrates argued that deviant behavior was not punishment by the gods but the result of . . .

5. ____________ was the name of the movement during the Middle Ages in which religious leaders searched out and killed those believed to be witches.

6. Briefly summarize present-day views about the people who were killed as witches during the Middle Ages.

7. The ____________ paradigm became prominent as an attempt to understand people who had lost sensory or motor abilities.

8. Mesmer used an early form of ____________ to treat people whose magnetic fluids were, he believed, out of balance.

9. What is the role of paradigms in science? to decide how methods showed be used

10. Langer & Abelson's study of clinician's watching a videotaped interview was used to show that . . .

people form different hypothesis
paradigms have influence

ANSWERS TO SELF-TEST, CHAPTER 1

MULTIPLE-CHOICE

1. C (p. 5-6)	2. A (p. 6)	3. A (p. 9)
4. B (p. 13)	5. C (p. 16)	6. D (p. 18)
7. D (p. 20)	8. C (p. 23)	9. C (p. 23)
10. D (p. 23)		

SHORT ANSWER

1. Tolerance for ambiguity (p. 5)

2. Clinical psychologist (p. 6)

3. The belief that the devil or other evil being controls the body to produce abnormal behavior (p. 7)

4. Natural causes (p. 8)

5. Inquisition (p. 10)

6. The prevailing view has been that they were mentally disturbed but new evidence suggests some "confessions" were the result of torture or trickery. (p. 11-12)

7. Psychogenic (p. 19)

8. Hypnotism (p. 20)

9. They define what concepts and methods the scientist uses. They specify assumptions used to study the world. (p. 22-23)

10. Paradigms influence how we make sense out of events. (p. 26)

2 Current Paradigms in Psychopathology and Therapy

OVERVIEW

This is the second of five introductory chapters over topics that are basic to the rest of the text. Chapter 1 discussed the role of paradigms in science and traced the paradigms that have been important in the history of psychopathology. Many of the differences underlying these paradigms are still unresolved. In particular, the relative importance of physical and psychological factors in pathology is still widely debated. As the field has developed, other distinctions have also emerged. These distinctions underly the current paradigms in psychopathology which are described in Chapter 2. These current paradigms will be used to help understand and study the various types of psychopathology described later. Thus the paradigms reappear many times throughout the rest of the text.

Chapters 3 and 4 will deal with the topics of classification and assessment. They describe the currently used categories of psychopathology and the methods used to assess individuals who may have psychological problems. There are a number of issues and controversies involved in both classifying pathology and assessing individuals. Not surprisingly these reflect differences between the various paradigms presented in Chapters 1 and 2.

Chapter 5 will discuss research methods in psychopathology. Then the text will begin covering the major forms of abnormality.

CHAPTER SUMMARY

Chapter 2 describes five current paradigms: the physiological, psychoanalytic, learning, cognitive, and humanistic paradigms. Each paradigm includes views on how we should understand, study, and treat psychopathology. As you study the chapter, remember that these are contemporary orientations. Thus you are likely to find your own ideas about psychopathology somewhere among them.

The Physiological Paradigm is similar to the so-called "medical model". This paradigm assumes that psychopathology, like medical disease, results from an organic problem. Thus we should try to identify and correct the defect - or at least control it's symptoms.

The Psychoanalytic Paradigm originated with Sigmund Freud who looked for psychological origins of psychopathology in repressed or unconscious processes originating in childhood conflicts. Present-day ego analysts are more concerned with conscious ego processes but continue the emphasis on using verbal techniques to lift repressions and re-examine the nature of conflicts.

Learning Paradigms, especially behaviorism, view psychopathology as abnormal behavior acquired through principles of classical conditioning, operant conditioning, and modeling. Thus the emphasis is on carefully defining terms and studying behavior in detail so that the the same conditioning principles can be used to acquire more effective behaviors.

The Cognitive Paradigm considers a more complex view of learning emphasizing how individuals organize stimuli into internal schema or organized networks of knowledge. Psychopathology is viewed in terms of ineffective understandings or irrational beliefs that may be relearned. Cognitive therapists share many beliefs and techniques with behavioral therapists.

The Humanistic Paradigm argues that people are inherently worthwhile and that psychopathology develops when people become afraid to accept their inner nature. Humanistic therapists encourage clients to rediscover and trust themselves and their impulses.

The Consequences of Adopting a Paradigm are to both focus and limit the search for answers. Fortunately there are many current paradigms in abnormal psychology since our understanding is very limited. A diathesis-stress paradigm may help integrate various viewpoints by focusing on underlying physical and psychological predispositions (diatheses) to react poorly to particular environmental stressors.

STUDY OBJECTIVES

After studying Chapter 2 you should know

1. The concept of "paradigm" and how it differs from a model.

2. The five major paradigms that are described as general explanations of psychopathology.

3. That the physiological paradigm assumes that the roots of psychopathology are somatic in nature, how this paradigm is distinguished from the medical model, and criticisms of the disease analogy in explaining "mental illness".

4. That the psychoanalytic paradigm traces psychopathology to unconscious conflicts based on Freud's ideas about the structure of the mind, the psychosexual stages of development, anxiety, and defenses.

5. That the learning paradigm asserts that abnormal behavior is learned much as normal behavior is learned, and about the three major learning process: Classical and Operant conditioning, and modeling.

6. That the learning view and the cognitive paradigm have much in common, although the latter places more emphasis

on unobservable processes and views the individual as an active participant in the learning process.

7. That the humanistic paradigm, developed in reaction to the dominance of the psychoanalytic and learning views, asserts the innate goodness of humans and the role of free will in their behavior.

8. That there are different therapeutic approaches that emanate from each paradigm.

9. That paradigms are both an aid and a limitation to scientific research and that no one paradigm adequately accounts for all of human behavior.

10. That the diathesis-stress paradigm is an attempt to integrate some of the seemingly contradictory views of differing paradigms.

11. That most psychologists do not align themselves with one school of thought, but instead say that they are eclectic - they pick the best aspects of different paradigms.

KEY TERMS

Physiological paradigm (p. 28)

Medical model (p. 28)

Psychoanalytic paradigm (p. 29)

Sigmund Freud (p. 29)

Id (p. 30)

Ego (p. 30 - 31)

Superego (p. 31)

Oral stage (p. 34)

Anal stage (p. 34)

Phallic stage (p. 34) 3-6

Latency (p. 34)

Genital stage (p. 34) final, adult stage

Fixation (p. 34) stuck in one stage

Neurotic anxiety (p. 34) fear of disasterous consequences that would follow a previously punished id impulse

Defense mechanism (p. 36)

Free association (p. 37)

Dream analysis (p. 37)

Analysis of defenses (p. 38) dispute the weak role that Freud assigned the ego.

Ivan Pavlov (p. 40) classical conditioning

Classical conditioning (p. 40)

UCS (p. 40) stimulus elicits response without prior learning

UCR (p. 40) response ↑

CS (p. 40) stimulus that is repeated

CR (p. 40) response followed by CS

Extinction (p. 40) CR is extinguished

B.F. Skinner (p. 42) All behavior determined by + & - reinforcements provided by the social environment

Reinforcement (p. 42) consequences

Operant conditioning (p. 42)

Shaping (p. 42) the desired operant behavior achieved by rewarding a series of responses.

Modeling (p. 42)

Systematic desensitization (p. 44)

Token economy (p. 46)

Modeling (p. 46)

Cognition (p. 46) group mental processes of perceiving, recognizing, conceiving, judging, reasoning
How people structure their experiences

Schema (p. 46)

Cognitive restructuring (p. 47)

Irrational beliefs (p. 48) people place excessive demands on themselves due to mistaken assumptions.

Humanistic paradigm (p. 48) human suffering comes from denial of this basic goodness

Self-actualization (p. 48)

Existential neurosis (p. 49) inability to exert free will + to seek fulfillment

Pre-morbid personality (p. 49) way of behaving the predisposes the ind. to the disorder. People's lives consist only of these acquired skills (eating, drinking, etc)

Carl Rogers (p. 50)

Client-centered therapy (p. 50) client responsible for most of the therapy

Unconditional positive regard (p. 50) acceptance + respect for the client's feelings + actions

Empathy (p. 50)

Diathesis-stress (p. 51)

Predisposition (p. 51)

STUDY QUESTIONS

THE PHYSIOLOGICAL PARADIGM (p. 28 - 29)

1. How is the " physiological paradigm" both A) similar to and B) different from the "medical model? (p. 28)

→ model implies concepts from 1 domain

medical diseases vary in causes + symptoms — implies a degree of precision that doesn't fit abn. behav.

paradigm looser sets of general assumptions about what, how should be studied

Physiological par.: a behavioral abnormality may be attributed to a disruption in one or more physiological processes

2. What is the assumption of the physiological paradigm's approach to treatment? Are physiological treatments based on knowledge that a problem is physiologically caused? Explain. (p. 28 - 29)

surgery or drugs that alter bodily functioning may be effective in treating or preventing abnormalities.

Some physiological interventions are not derived from knowledge of the cause.

THE PSYCHOANALYTIC PARADIGM (p. 29 - 38)

3. Briefly describe Freud's three structures of the mind and his four (or five) stages of psychosexual development. (p. 29 - 34)

id
ego (6 mos) reality principle
superego moral judgements

oral
anal
phallic (genitalia)
latency
genital

4. Summarize Freud's two theories of neurotic anxiety. Explain how each theory proposes we deal with conflicts between our impulses and our fears about the consequences of acting on them. (p. 34 - 35) (ANXIOUS FROM WANTS WE DON'T GET)

① stemmed from blockage of unconscious impulses that are repressed
② anxiety about impulses signals need for their repression (ANXIOUS BECAUSE WE FEAR OUR WANTS); involves surrounding situations

5. What is the aim of psychoanalytic therapy and why? Describe three methods used by psychoanalysts. (p. 37 - 38) Attempts to remove earlier repression - face childhood conflict & resolve in light of adult reality
Repression has prevented the ego from growing.

free association
dream analysis

LEARNING PARADIGMS (p. 38 - 46)

6. What methods did early behaviorism oppose? What alternative did it offer? (p. 38 - 40)

Opposed introspection
classical conditioning
Operant " (law of effect)

- abnormality is a relativistic concept
- increased observation

7. Describe three basic learning paradigms. Give examples of each. (p. 40 - 43)

Classical Conditioning

Operant Conditioning - the effect of consequences on behavior "law of effect"

modeling

8. What are two assumption of all learning points of view regarding deviant behavior? How effective have learning views been in (1) improving observations and (2) finding causes for abnormality? (p. 43)

① ABNORMAL BEHAVIOR IS LEARNED

② ABNORMALITY IS RELATIVISTIC - labeling is linked to a social context

9. Describe a behavior therapy procedure which is based on each of the three learning paradigms. (p. 43 - 46)

counterconditioning ?

THE COGNITIVE PARADIGM (p. 46 - 48)

10. How does the cognitive paradigm view the learning process? As an example of cognitive behavior therapy briefly summarize Ellis' rational-emotive approach. (p. 46 - 48)

learning process is much more complex than forming stimulus-response associations.

"irrational beliefs" put excessive demands on one's self
"rational-emotive" help to overcome ↑

11. Describe the similarities between learning and cognitive paradigms in approach to therapy and in philosophy (p. 48)

~~cognitive~~ Changing behavioral techniques is the most powerful way to enhance self-efficacy.

Clients should behave in ways that were before blocked by negative thoughts

THE HUMANISTIC PARADIGM (p. 48 - 50)

12. Summarize the humanistic view of human behavior in four points. (Hint: look for human nature, reason for problems, phenomenological world, and free will.) (p. 48 - 49)

Human nature is basically good; therefore, problems develop when outside evaluations + expectations are a concern instead of following one's own innate drives.

Each has an internal frame of reference from past experience.

Free will: humans initiate action instead of being passive about the environ. or internal id imp.

13. Summarize the idea of existential neurosis and the kind of people who may develop it? How is existential neurosis an example of the humanistic approach to psychopathology? (p. 49

- Inability to exert free will / seek fulfillment
People who merely conform to society instead of creating a personal destiny

14. Why do humanistic therapists try to avoid telling their clients what to do? Why do they try to have unconditional positive regard and empathy? (p. 49 - 50)

Clients should get in touch w. inner selves
Clients will begin to talk in a more honest & emotional way about themselves; gain access to basic healthy inner natures.

CONSEQUENCES OF ADOPTING A PARADIGM (p. 50 - 54)

15. What does the text see as consequences of adopting a paradigm? Explain the diathesis-stress paradigm and how it may be extended to make current paradigms more flexible. (p. 50 - 54)

makes a prior decision / possibilities & info may be overlooked

SELF-TEST, CHAPTER 2

MULTIPLE CHOICE

1. Many people talk in terms of mental "patients" who are "cured" in mental "hospitals". The text suggests that our use of such terms reflects the fact that:
   - A. Medical model thinking is pervasive in society
   - B. We depend on physicians to help people
   - C. We need better words to describe such people
   - D. We use circular reasoning to describe mental illness

2. According to Freud, in each stage of psychosexual development the individual must:
   - A. Learn to express his or her sexual urges
   - B. Strive to become more and more self-actualized
   - C. Deal with a specific kind of conflict
   - D. Avoid involvement in the Oedipus complex

3. The critical assumption of the (so called) medical model of abnormal psychology is that:
   - A. Mental illness is caused by germs
   - B. Abnormal behavior is like a disease
   - C. Only physicians are qualified to treat abnormality
   - D. Abnormality can only be understood from the phenomenological world of the patient

4. According to Freud the id, ego, and super-ego are:
   - A. Physical parts of the brain
   - B. Three innate or biological drives
   - C. Not present at birth
   - D. Functions of the personality

5. In Freudian theory "neurotic anxiety" results from:
   - A. Not taking time to relax from daily pressures
   - B. Fear of expressing instinctual impulses
   - C. Not living up to one's own moral standards
   - D. Guilt over past misdeeds

6. What form of learning is illustrated by this example. Joe, who hasn't spoken for months, walks up to his therapist one day and says "Hello". The therapist praises Joe lavishly. An hour later Joe is observed wandering around saying "Hello" to everyone.
   A. Classical
   B. Operant
   C. Modeling
   D. Cognitive

7. The crucial assumption of behavioral therapies is that abnormal behavior
   A. Is basically different from normal behavior
   B. Can only be understood by looking at the whole person
   C. Is learned like most other behaviors
   D. Results from repressed childhood experiences

8. In humanistic therapy the concept of ____________ means that each person's problems can only be understood in terms of their own internal way of understanding life
   A. Phenomenological world
   B. Existential neurosis
   C. Irrational beliefs
   D. Free association

9. A therapist following the _________ paradigm would most value expressing unconditional positive regard.
   A. Psychoanalytic
   B. Learning
   C. Cognitive
   D. Humanistic

Carl Rogers

10. The fact that many paradigms exist in abnormal psychology is ___________ because ______________
   A. Undesirable, many are outdated and relatively useless
   B. Undesirable, they keep us from being scientifically objective
   C. Desirable, they show that our knowledge is sophisticated
   D. Desirable, they give us many ways to study human problems

SHORT ANSWER

1. Why does the text prefer the term "physiological paradigm" to "medical model"?

2. Define "ego".

3. List, in order, Freud's stages of development.

4. In the Freudian technique of ____________ patients are to say whatever comes into their mind without censoring anything.

5. The snake would be considered a ____________ in a classical conditioning analysis of the following. Little Judy was walking with her father when they saw a snake. Judy started to walk up to it but her father screamed "A snake!" and dragged her away scaring her. Now, when Judy sees a snake, she cries and runs away.

6. In the behavioral technique of ____________ individuals are taught to relax deeply. Then, while relaxed, they imagine situations which are increasingly anxiety provoking.

7. Cognitive psychologists are interested in what kinds of questions?

8. Maddi suggests that existential neurosis may develop in individuals who have not (done what?) . . .

9. The following is an example of the ____________ paradigm. College students become anxious if their parents pushed them very hard to make good grades and if they then take very difficult courses.

10. Define "Diathesis"

ANSWERS TO SELF-TEST, CHAPTER 2

MULTIPLE-CHOICE

1. A (p. 28)
2. C (p. 29)
3. B (p. 29)
4. D (p. 29,34)
5. B (p. 29-30)
6. B (p. 42)
7. C (p. 43)
8. A (p. 49)
9. D (p. 50)
10. D (p. 51

SHORT ANSWER

1. Because "medical model" is vague. Arguments often reduce to whether behavior is due to physiological processes. (p. 28-29)

2. In psychoanalysis, the part of the personality that deals with reality and mediates between reality and inner urges (p. 30)

3. Oral, Anal, Phallic, (latency period - not a stage), Genital. (p. 34)

4. Free association (p. 37)

5. Conditioned stimulus (p. 40)

6. Systematic desensitization (p. 44-46)

7. How do we interpret experiences or make sense out of situations. (p. 46-47)

8. Developed their own values, goals, and views on life. (p. 49)

9. Diathesis-stress. (p. 51)

10. A predisposition (physiological or psychological) to develop a problem. (p. 51)

3 Classification and Diagnosis

OVERVIEW

This is the third of five introductory chapters. The first two chapters covered historical and contemporary paradigms or theories of abnormality. The remaining three deal with less theoretical issues. Chapter 3 summarizes the standard diagnostic system for classifying disturbed individuals and then goes on to discuss some basic issues regarding classification. Chapter 4 deals with issues and methods of assessing individuals in order to classify or, more generally, to understand their problems. Chapter 5 will cover research methods and will complete the introductory chapters.

Chapters 3, 4, and 5 are less overtly theoretical than the earlier chapters. Still, the paradigm differences continue and are reflected in differences about how best to classify and study abnormality.

CHAPTER SUMMARY

Chapter 3 discusses the standard system for categorizing psychopathology and issues concerning this system and classification in general.

<u>DSM-III - The Diagnostic System of the American Psychiatric Association</u> summarizes the history and some general characteristics of the standard system especially it's

approach of diagnosing individuals on multiple axes or dimensions. The chapter summarizes the main categories in DSM-III. Later chapters will cover these categories in detail.

Issues in the Classification of Abnormal Behavior are whether people should be classified at all and whether DSM-III is a good classification system. In classifying we lose information, the similarities between normal and abnormal, and may stigmatize people. However some classification system is needed in order to study and treat problems. Earlier DSM systems were criticized for lack of reliability (consistency in applying labels) and validity (accuracy of the labels). DSM-III appears more reliable but it's broader utility is not yet clear.

STUDY OBJECTIVES

After studying Chapter 3 you should know

1. That DSM III is quite different from earlier classification systems and that it's multiaxial structure is perhaps its most distinctive innovation.

2. That the range of mental disorders listed in DSM-III are of such great importance that they form the basis for organizing much of the text.

3. That some critics object to the very concept of classifying abnormal behavior and the reasons for their objections.

4. That other critics see value in classifying abnormal behavior, but question the reliability and validity of past and current classification systems.

5. That diagnostic reliability refers to whether or not different diagnosticians will agree on a given diagnosis.

6. That the validity of a classification is measured (in three ways) by whether or not accurate statements and predictions can be made from knowledge of class materials.

7. That validity is dependent upon reliability because the more unreliable a diagnosis is, the more difficult it is to establish its validity.

8. That although DSM-III is more reliable than its predecessors because it contains specific diagnostic criteria, it is still far from perfect.

KEY TERMS

DSM-III (p. 56)

Multiaxial classification (p. 56)

Disorders Usually First Evident in Infancy, Childhood, or Adolescence (p. 58)

Organic Mental Disorders (p. 58)

Substance Use Disorders (p. 59)

Schizophrenic Disorders (p. 59)

Paranoid Disorders (p. 59)

Affective Disorders (p. 59)

Anxiety Disorders (p. 59)

Somatoform Disorders (p. 60)

Dissociative Disorders (p. 60)

Psychosexual Disorders (p. 60)

Psychological Factors Affecting Physical Conditions (p. 60)

Personality Disorders (p. 60)

Specific Developmental Disorders (p. 60)

Reliability (p. 62)

Validity (p. 64)

Etiological validity (p. 64)

Concurrent validity (p. 64)

Predictive validity (p. 64)

I. Disorders evident in infancy, early childhood
II. Personality disorders
III. Physical conditions
IV. Severity of Psychosocial stressors
V. Adaptive functioning ~ past yr.

STUDY QUESTIONS

DSM-III - THE DIAGNOSTIC SYSTEM OF THE AMERICAN PSYCHIATRIC ASSOCIATION (p. 56 - 60)

1. What is "DSM-III" and who publishes it? (p. 56)

Adopts descriptive approach
defines in observational terms rather than theoretical
multi-axial
3 dimensions of behavior that are coded

2. How are individuals diagnosed in DSM-III's "multiaxial" system. What are the five axes and the rationale for distinguishing them (especially axes I and II)? (p. 56 - 57)

each individual is rated on five separate dimensions
Broad range of info must be considered due to 5 axes. (axes)
Axis I: includes all categories except for personality + specific developmental disorders
I + II comprise the classification of abn. behavior.

3. Identify and define the labels that comprise axes I and II (13 in all). (You may wish to refer to the glossary in the back of the text.) (p. 58 - 60)

1. Disorders of early childhood
2. Organic mental disorders
3. Substance use disorders
4. Schizo
5. paranoid
6. affective
7. anxiety
8. somatoform
9. dissociative
10. psychosexual
11. Psych factors affecting phys. cond.
12. personality
13. development disorders

ISSUES IN THE CLASSIFICATION OF ABNORMAL BEHAVIOR (p. 60 - 66)

4. What two general issues in the classification of abnormal behavior does the text identify? (p. 60 - 61)

① Classification is irrelevant to field of abn. behavior
-there is a continuum ranging from adjustment to maj

② specific deficiencies in the way diagnoses are made are found

5. Summarize three issues regarding regarding classification per.se. What general defense of classification is offered? (p. 61 - 62)

① Whenever a person is classified info is lost & the person's uniqueness is overlooked; people may be grouped on a trivial basis while imp. differences are ignored

② Does not allow the continuity between normal & abn. behavior to be considered

③ stigmatizes

6. Distinguish between "reliability" and "validity". Summarize Beck et al.'s (1962) study on the reliability of DSM. (p. 62 - 64)

reliability: whether or not a test or measurement system produces the same results every time.

validity: whether or not accurate statements/predictions can be made about a class once formed

7. What three kinds of validity may be sought for a diagnosis? (p. 64 - 65)

<u>etiological</u>: same historical antecedents have caused the disorder

<u>Concurrent</u>: other symptoms that aren't part of the diagnosis are discovered

Predictive: similar future behavior on the part of the patients suffering from it.

8. How did DSM-III attempt to respond to the criticisms above? What three problems (may) remain? (p. 65 - 66)

basis for making diagnosis are much more detailed & concrete

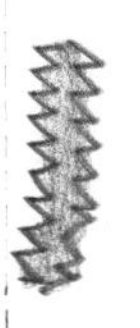

- rules for making diagnostic decisions are unclear
- diagnosticians may not always adhere precisely to the criteria
- diagnoses made may not reveal anything useful (causes bias & clinicians own judgements to take over

SELF-TEST, CHAPTER 3

MULTIPLE-CHOICE

1. DSM-III is published by the
   A. American Psychiatric Association
   B. American Psychological Association
   C. World Health Organization
   D. United States Government

2. DSM-III is "multiaxial" which means that it
   A. Can be used to diagnose many kinds of psychopathology
   B. Calculates the multiple effect of many factors in order to arrive at a diagnosis
   C. Classifies an individual on each of several dimensions
   D. Can be used by individuals in many different professions

3. In DSM-III ____________ disorders involve sudden alterations in consciousness affecting memory and identity such as amnesia.
   A. Somatoform
   B. Affective
   C. Dissociative
   D. Personality

4. Which of the following is NOT raised by those who oppose classification in general?
   A. Classifying causes us to lose information about the unique qualities of the individual.
   B. Classification is based on unproven assumptions of the medical model
   C. Classification ignores the continuity between normal and abnormal behavior
   D. Classification schemes encourage us to see pathology everywhere

5. The text points out that information about the individual which is lost in classifying
   - A. Is usually very limited
   - B. Is often vital in understanding the individual's problem
   - C. May or may not be relevant depending on the purpose of classifying
   - D. Must always be preserved according to recent court rulings

6. It is desirable to classify people with psychological problems, despite problems with our classification system, because
   - A. Understanding differences between problems is important in studying and treating them
   - B. The same problem may effect individuals differently and treatment can be adjusted to the individual
   - C. Some problems require that people with them be institutionalized for their own protection
   - D. Accurate diagnoses are required by insurance companies before they pay for treatment

7. Which of the following is identified by the text as a general issue in the classification of abnormal behavior?
   - A. Is there such a thing as abnormality?
   - B. Whether or not animal research applies to human abnormality
   - C. What professions are qualified to diagnose abnormality
   - D. Is DSM a good system for classifying abnormality

8. A group of diagnosticians who always gave the same label to all their patients regardless of their complaints would have
   - A. Validity but not reliability
   - B. Reliability but not validity
   - C. Both reliability and validity
   - D. Neither reliability nor validity

9. The diagnostic reliability and validity of DSM-III was (hopefully) improved over that of earlier editions by
   A. Insuring that all paradigms were represented among its' authors
   B. Providing extensive field training for diagnosticians using it
   C. Eliminating overlapping and rarely used categories
   D. Including more explicit and extensive descriptions of categories

10. The text criticizes DSM-III for
   A. Allowing subjective factors and biases to play a role in diagnosis
   B. Overly restricting the number of possible diagnoses
   C. Not paying attention to problems of reliability
   D. Making rules for arriving at diagnoses needlessly complex

SHORT ANSWER

1. In DSM-III axis II is used to designate

2. In DSM-III ____________ are characterized by long-term, inflexible, maladaptive patterns of behavior.

3. Define and give an example of "Affective disorders".

4. The two major groups of issues in the classification of abnormal behavior are ____________ and ____________.

5. One possible criticism of classifying people is that it is difficult to indicate degrees of abnormality because . . .

6. A diagnostic label is ____________ if diagnosticians agree on applying it to particular individuals.

7. What was the most common reason for disagreements between diagnosticians in the study by Back and others?

Inadequacies in diagnostic system

8. The validity of a diagnostic label is always limited by its reliability.

9. A diagnostic label is said to have etiological validity if . . .

same historical causes

10. In evaluating the reliability and validity of DSM-III the text concludes that. . .

reliable but validity unclear

ANSWERS TO SELF-TEST, CHAPTER 3

MULTIPLE-CHOICE

1. A (p. 56)
2. C (p. 56-57)
3. C (p. 60)
4. B (p. 60-61)
5. C (p. 61)
6. A (p. 61-62)
7. D (p. 62)
8. B (p. 62-65)
9. D (p. 65)
10. A (p. 66)

SHORT ANSWER

1. Long term problems such as personality disorders and specific developmental disorders. (p. 56-57)

2. Personality disorders. (p. 60)

3. Disturbances of mood such as depression or mania. (p. 59)

4. The relevance of classification per se. Criticisms of actual diagnostic practices. (p. 60 & 62)

5. The labels are discrete entities (that is, people either are or are not labeled.) (p. 61)

6. Reliable (p. 62)

7. Inadequacies in the diagnostic system. (p. 62)

8. Validity. Reliability. (p. 64)

9. The same historical causes are found in individuals given the label. (p. 64)

10. It is more reliable but it's validity remains unclear. (p. 65-66)

4 Clinical Assessment Procedures

OVERVIEW

This is the fourth of five introductory chapters over basic issues in psychopathology. The first two chapters covered historical and contemporary paradigms or theories of abnormality. Chapter 3 dealt with DSM-III, the standard system for classifying abnormality, and then went on to summarize general issues regarding classification.

This chapter will cover the major methods used to assess and classify behavior as well as issues underlying these methods. The issues involve both paradigm differences (discussed in Chapters 1 and 2) and issues of reliability and validity (discussed in Chapter 3).

Chapter 5 will cover research methods and will complete the introductory chapters. Research issues have been included in earlier chapters (and will appear throughout the text). Chapter 5 pulls these issues together by showing the relative strengths and limitations of various research approaches.

CHAPTER SUMMARY

Chapter 4 describes methods of assessing individuals and their problems in order to develop appropriate treatment programs. The first three sections describe basic assessment procedures.

Personality Assessment covers the traditional assessment methods: clinical interviews, personality tests including projective tests and objective personality inventories, and intelligence tests. The chapter describes each method and then discusses problems in using it. The problems concern both the paradigms underlying these methods and problems with the reliability and validity of the methods. (Intelligence tests are covered in detail in Chapter 16)

Assessment of Brain Abnormalities describes both medical (tomographic X-Ray scanning)) and neuropsychological methods of assessing brain damage. Again both the methods and limitations of these procedures are described.

Behavioral Assessment procedures gather information using an SORC model. Four behavioral methods are described: direct observation, interviews & self-reports, cognitive assessment and physiological measures. Based on the behavioral paradigm, these procedures look for specific individual responses to particular situations rather than global or underlying traits as do the traditional methods above. Behaviorists hope that studying specific problem behaviors will lead them more directly to procedures for changing the behaviors. Reliability and validity issues in behavioral assessment are discussed.

Behavioral assessment methods bring up the issue of whether people's actions are the result of underlying traits or the particular situation. The Consistency and Variability of Behavior focuses directly on this issue.

STUDY OBJECTIVES

After studying Chapter 4 you should know

1. That the clinical interview is a widely used assessment method usually involving observation of interviewee responses and establishing rapport. The content of the interview is largely unstructured and dependent upon the the interviewer's paradigm.

2. That projective tests are deliberately made to be ambiguous so that the testee may project onto the stimulus material. The unstructured nature of these tests raises questions concerning validity and reliability.

3. That personality inventories are highly structures tests, but they are limited by various problems with self-report data.

4. That because certain relationships between behavior and brain structures are known, neurological tests can reveal information about the sites of brain damage.

5. That behavioral assessment is more concerned with situational specificity, whereas traditional assessment emphasizes traits or behavioral consistency.

6. That although observational assessment is the hallmark of the behavioral approach, self-report, cognition, and psychophysiological measures also are used.

7. That in addition to an emphasis on situational specificity, behavioral assessment is more treatment focused and more direct than other forms of assessment.

8. That, as with other forms of assessment, the problems of reliability and validity plague behavioral assessment.

9. That cognitive, behavioral, and physiological measures often do not correlate with one another.

10. That the debate continues as to whether people are consistent in their behavior across situations or whether behavior is situation specific.

KEY TERMS

Assessment procedures (p. 68)

Clinical interview (p. 68)

Rapport (p. 68) Close relationship

Standardization (p. 69)

Projective technique (p. 69) Rorschach inkblot, TAT
set of standard stimuli

Projective hypothesis (p. 71)

Personality inventories (p. 73)
indicate whether or not statements do or don't apply to them

Intelligence test (p. 75)

Neuropsychological test (p. 76)

Situational determinants (vs. traits) (p. 77)

Behav. SORC (p. 78) S-stimuli R-overt responses
O-organismic C-consequent var.-after reinforcement

Self-monitoring (p. 79)

Reactivity (p. 79)

Psychophysiology (p. 84)

External validity (p. 88) whether the assessment applies to real-world situations.

Rosenthal effect (p. 89) experimental bias

STUDY QUESTIONS

PERSONALITY ASSESSMENT (p. 68 - 75)

1. Describe five factors which influence the results of a clinical interview. (p. 68 - 69)

   ① skill of interviewer (rapport)
   ② empathy statements (accepting attitude)
   ③ situational factors appropriate
   ④ (how interviews are structured
   (how info is collected

2. What is the basic idea (the projective hypothesis) behind projective personality tests? What do we know about their validity? (p. 69 - 72)

   stimulus materials are unstructured so patient's response will be determined by unconscious processes / own attitudes, (motivations, modes will be (revealed.
   low validity : poor job of differentiating normal from (neurotic + diff. between mentally ill.

3. How are personality inventories (especially the MMPI) developed and refined into "scales" (three steps)? What are two kinds of problems with inventories and how are they handled? (p. 73 - 74)

   ① rely on factual info
   clinicians provided no. statements that indicated mental prob.
   ② items rated as self-descriptive (not by people already diagnosed)
   ③ items that discriminated were (retained

   if the ind. answered a large no. the same way as the diagnostic group, behavior was expected *(resemble

- Tests can be faked
- Social desirability factors in

4. What are/were intelligence tests designed to measure? (Is this your understanding of the term "intelligence"?) What two points does the text stress in evaluating these tests? (p. 75)

predict which children needed special schooling

① tests only measure what a psychologist considers intelligence to be

② tests predict who will succeed in ed. system

ASSESSMENT OF BRAIN ABNORMALITIES (p. 75 - 77)

5. Why are neuropsychological tests of brain abnormalities needed? Describe, in general, these tests and how they are used. (p. 76 - 77)

Tactual Performance Test: fit shapes into board w/ blindfolded
Trail Making
Finger Oscillation - depress keys while timed
Category
Aphasia Screening: lang. abilities

BEHAVIORAL ASSESSMENT (p. 77 - 90)

6. Explain how paradigm differences lead behaviorists to on situational determinants rather than traits as the causes of behavior? Describe the behavioral (SORC) approach to assessment. (p. 77 - 78)

Env. conditions precede & follow certain responses
focus on " under which behavior does/'nt occur

S- Stimuli: precede prob
O- organismic: physiological + psychological
R- overt responses (determine what beh. is problematic)
C- consequent variables (appear to reinforce behavior)

7. Describe four methods of behavioral assessment. Some of these methods are also used in non-behavioral assessment. Be sure to describe the particular ways in which behaviorists have used them. (p. 78 - 84)

Direct observation
Interviews / self-report
Cognitive assessment
physiological measurement

8. How does behavioral assessment differ from traditional approaches in its relationship to treatment or behavior change procedures? Give an example of this. (p. 84 - 86)

search for situational determinants of behavior

9. Why has the reliability and validity of behavioral assessment not been widely studied? Identify two factors that influence the reliability and four factors that influence the validity of behavioral measures. (p. 86 - 90)

THE CONSISTENCY AND VARIABILITY OF BEHAVIOR (p. 90 - 91)

10. Summarize Mischel's and Wachtel's position on the determinants of behavior. How conclusive is the evidence so far? (p. 90 - 91)

Mischel: env. more important than personality traits
people will behave consistently in a variety of situations

Wachtel: people perceive certain situations in a partic. fashion
responses can be elicited from surroundings

SELF-TEST, CHAPTER 4

MULTIPLE-CHOICE

1. In clinical interviewing "rapport" refers to
   A. The particular paradigm of the interviewer
   B. The degree to which the interview is structures
   C. Paying attention to how the person answers questions
   D. Having a close trusting relationship

2. One major problem in using projective personality tests is that
   A. During interpretation unconscious factors are easily ignored
   B. The validity of many popular responses is unproven
   C. Interpretation relies heavily on cognitive theories
   D. Most people can easily falsify their responses

3. One step in the process of developing personality inventories such as the MMPI is to
   A. Identify items that people with a specific problem answer differently
   B. Select stimuli which are ambiguous to most people
   C. Eliminate items that are too obvious in their content
   D. Analyze preliminary results using the SORC model

4. Psychological tests of organic brain dysfunction are needed because.
   A. Physical measures are too expensive
   B. Brain dysfunction is an important cause of many psychological problems.
   C. Medical tests can not detect subtle abnormalities
   D. Brain dysfunctions often alter performance on personality tests
   E. They provide an important source of income for psychologists

5. Which of the following is LEAST likely to be used in behavioral assessment
   A. Self-report inventories
   B. Interviews
   C. Physiological measures
   D. Projective tests

6. In cognitive assessment there has been much research aimed at studying peoples' cognitions
   A. Using direct psychophysiological measurements
   B. While they are being confronted with particular situations
   C. When faced with ambiguous stimuli such as inkblots
   D. About the specific assessment procedures themselves

7. Behavioral assessment differs from traditional assessment approaches in that
   A. It is closely tied to treatment
   B. It uses psychological tests
   C. It has proven effective in identifying causes of abnormality
   D. Anxiety can be measured directly

8. The validity of behavioral assessment procedures has been
   A. Relatively independent of the reliability of the procedures
   B. Similar to that of non-behavioral procedures
   C. Assumed by researchers until recently
   D. Difficult to study because of the many inferences involved

9. "The consistency and variability of behavior" is an argument over the relative importance of ____________ and ____________ in abnormality.
   A. Research and clinical insight
   B. Physiology and psychology
   C. Traits and environment
   D. Reliability and validity

10. In the debate over the consistency and variability of behavior psychodynamic trait theorists have argued that
- (A.) Disturbed individuals may behave more consistently than normals
- B. Behaviorists have averaged behavior across too many situations
- C. Consistency can only be inferred from the individual's internal frame of reference
- D. Behaviorists have failed to study internal thought processes

SHORT ANSWER

1. In the process of standardization test norms are established based on the responses people make to the test.

2. Define "projective hypothesis".

people react to stimuli in their own way thus their motivations & unconscious is shown

3. What type of items are used in lie scales of personality inventories such as the MMPI?

people might want to be labeled as but can't do so honestly.

4. Intelligence tests are designed to measure or predict . .

success in education system

5. What is the rationale for selecting the behaviors measured by neuropsychological tests?

behaviors related to certain brain structures.

6. Traditional assessment concentrates on personality while behavioral assessment concentrates on situational determinates of behavior.

7. In the method of "direct observation of behavior" behavioral therapists not only watch the behavior but also . . .

analyze

8. Behavioral therapists may use physiological measures in order to get a more complete picture of emotional responses to situations.

9. The reliability of behavioral assessment has been shown to depend on the complexity of the task and the conscientiousness of the observers.

10. The external of a behavioral assessment refers to whether the assessment applies to the real-world situations of interest.

ANSWERS TO SELF-TEST, CHAPTER 4

MULTIPLE-CHOICE

1. D (p. 68) 2. B (p. 72) 3. A (p. 73)
4. C (p. 76) 5. D (p. 79,84) 6. B (p. 81)
7. A (p. 84) 8. C (p. 87) 9. C (p. 90)
10. A (p. 91)

SHORT ANSWER

1. Standardization (p. 69)

2. An individual's responses to unstructured stimuli are determined by unconscious personality processes. (p. 71)

3. Items that people might like to endorse but cannot do so honestly (p. 73-74)

4. Who will succeed in school. (p. 75)

5. Select behaviors known to be related to particular brain structures. (p. 76-77)

6. Personality structures or traits (p. 77)

7. Analyze the sequences using behavioral terms or concepts. (p. 78-79)

8. Physiological measures (p. 84)

9. Reliability (p. 86-87)

10. External or ecological validity (p. 88)

5 Research Methods in the Study of Abnormal Behavior

OVERVIEW

Earlier chapters have covered paradigms or theories in psychopathology (Chapters 1 & 2) and classification and assessment issues (Chapters 3 & 4). Chapter 5 discusses scientific methods and research designs in abnormal psychology.

Many research issues have already been mentioned in Chapters 1 thru 4. In fact, it may have seemed that scientific research creates more confusion than answers. Research can be complex, at least in part because researchers are very concerned about the limitations of their approach and their methods. It is said that there is no perfect research design. Each has both strengths and limitations. Chapter 5 provides a background for understanding the research evidence regarding various problem behaviors in the chapters to come.

Chapter 5 is the last introductory chapter. Chapter 6 begins the first of several parts of the text which discuss various specific forms of abnormality.

CHAPTER SUMMARY

Chapter 5 discusses the methods scientists use to develop systematic knowledge as a basis for developing and evaluating theories and principles.

Science and Scientific Methods identifies basic principles of science. Statements and ideas must be publicly testable and able to be proven false. Observations must be reliable or repeatable. Theories are propositions which both result from research and generate testable ideas for further research.

The Research Methods of Abnormal Psychology include case studies, correlational studies, and three forms of experiments. These methods vary in the kind of data they produce and way in which inferences, especially inferences about causes, can be drawn.

The case study is an extensive description of a particular, often unusual, problem or procedure. Case studies can provide useful descriptions and suggest hypotheses for further research. It is difficult to develop general principles from them but they can provide examples to disconfirm principles.

Correlational methods measure the relationship between two (or more) variables (for example between course grades and anxiety). They are widely used in abnormal psychology but, because they do not change variables, it is difficult draw conclusions about causation from them.

In experiments one (or more) independent variables are actually changed and the effects of the change on dependent variable(s) are studied. Experiments are preferred for studying causation. However in abnormal psychology many variables cannot be manipulated for practical or ethical reasons. Features of experimental designs are described. Variables may be manipulated using control groups, single-subjects, or mixed designs.

STUDY OBJECTIVES

After studying Chapter 5 you should know

1. Science is the pursuit of systematized knowledge through observation, although it is not purely objective and is influenced by time and convention.

2. In order to be considered scientific, theories must be testable or falsifiable and reliable.

3. That the case study lacks control and objectivity, but it can be useful for 1) describing unusual phenomena, 2) disconfirming supposedly universal aspects of a theory and, 3) generating hypothesis.

4. That the correlational method is a valuable means of systematically studying the association between two or more variables, but third variables and reverse causality interpretations prohibit causal inference.

5. That statistical significance refers to a convention adopted by scientists wherein a finding is not considered to be reliable unless the odds are less than 5 in 100 that it occurred by chance. Statistical significance does not guarantee social significance.

6. That the experiment, when properly conducted, is a powerful tool for determining causality, although ethical and practical problems often prohibit the use of the experiment as a means of studying psychopathology.

7. That the basic features of the experiment include the experimental hypothesis, independent variables, dependent variables, experimental effects, control groups, and random assignment.

8. That internal validity refers to whether the results obtained can be confidently attributed to the independent variable, and that external validity concerns whether the results of a particular study are generalizable.

9. That analogue experiments are frequently used to study psychopathology and that caution must be used in making various analogies.

10. That diagnosis is a classificatory variable and all comparisons made between groups of patients with different diagnoses are correlation studies.

KEY TERMS

Theory (p. 94) set of propositions meant to explain a class of phenomena

Case study (p. 96) lack degree of control & objectivity
1) provide detailed description 2) disconfirm universal theoretical proposition

Idiographic (p. 99)
investigative procedures that consider unique charact. of 1 3) generate hypothesis to test

Nomothetic (p. 99)
abstract / to formulation of general laws that explain a wide range of phenomena

Correlational method (p. 99)
whether there is a relationship between 2 or more variables

Correlation coefficient (r) (p. 99)

Statistical significance (p. 100)
the likelihood that the obtained relationship happened by chance & would be unlikely to happen again

Classificatory variable (p. 101)
subjects bring in (sex, age, etc.)

Directionality problem (p. 102)
difficulty in correlational research (2 variables are related unclear of cause)

Third variable problem (p. 102)
neither variable causes the other

The experiment (p. 102) most powerful for determining causal relationships

Experimental hypothesis (p. 103)

Independent variable (p. 103)
can be manipulated
under control of experimenter

Dependent variable (p. 103) depends on independent

Experimental effect (p. 103) Differences in groups are found to be a function of variations in the ind't variable

Internal validity (p. 104) extent to which experimental results can be attributed to man. of ind't variable

Control group (p. 104) subjects in experiment for whom the the ind't variable isn't manipulated

Confounds (p. 104) confound results, impossible to interpret

Random assignment (p. 104) ensuring that every subject has same chance of being assigned to any group

Double-blind (p. 104)

External validity (p. 105) results of any piece of research can be generalized beyond the immediate experiment

Analogue experiment (p. 105) experiment different from but related to actual interest of experimenter

Single-subject design (p. 106) include reversal & multiple-baseline designs in operant research.

Reversal (ABAB) design (p. 107)

Multiple-baseline design (p. 107) 2 or more behaviors selected for study.

Mixed design (p. 108)

Subjects that can be divided into 2 or more discrete & nonoverlapping populations are assigned as groups to each experimental condition

STUDY QUESTIONS

SCIENCE AND SCIENTIFIC METHODS (p. 94 - 95)

1. Explain three contemporary criteria for evaluating scientific observations and explanations. (Notice that the third involves three points.) (p. 94 - 95)

Testability
Reliability
Theory - explain phenomena

THE RESEARCH METHODS OF ABNORMAL PSYCHOLOGY (p. 95 - 109)

2. What is done in a case study? Explain three ways in which case studies are useful. (p. 96 - 99)

usefulness
1) provide detailed description
2) disconfirm universal theoretical proposition
3) generate hypothesis

3. What kind of questions do correlational methods ask? How are the results expressed and their importance evaluated? (p. 99 - 100)

asked concerning relationships

r + positively related

r - neg. rel.
one variable increases - other decreases

4. Identify and explain the advantages and disadvantages of correlational methods as applied to psychopathology (p. 101 - 102)

5. Identify four basic features of the experimental design. How is this method different from the correlational method? (p. 102 - 103)

experimenter hypothesis
independent variable
dependent "
experimental effect

6. Describe how "control groups", "random assignment", and "double-blinds" are used to eliminate "confounds" and secure "internal validity" (p. 104 - 105)

7. What is "external validity" and why is it difficult to demonstrate? (p. 105)

knowing that one is a subject in an experiment alters behavior

results from animals gen. to humans

Best that can be done is perform similar studies in new settings w/ new participants

8. What is an analogue experiment? What is the advantage and the disadvantage of using analogues in experimental designs? (p. 105 - 106)

9. Describe two major types of single-subject experimental designs? In what way is it difficult to generalize the results of single-subject research? (p. 106 - 108)

10. What is a mixed design? Identify an advantage and a disadvantage of mixed designs (p. 108 - 109)

SELF-TEST, CHAPTER 5

MULTIPLE-CHOICE

1. In science "falsifiability" means that
    A. Scientific theories rarely apply in all situations
    B. Research must be guided by theories
    C. Ideas must be capable of being proven wrong
    D. Research results can be distorted or misleading

2. In science theories are commonly used to
    A. Generate ideas for future research
    B. Account for observed relationships
    C. Bridge temporal gaps between concepts
    D. All of the above

3. What experimental design is illustrated by the following; A therapist describes in great detail a particular patient and the innovative procedures she used to successfully treat him
    A. Case history
    B. Correlational method
    C. Experiment
    D. Single-subject research
    E. Mixed design

4. Case studies can be of great value in
    A. Comparing the effectiveness of treatments
    B. Suggesting possibilities for further research
    C. Demonstrating causal relationships
    D. Conducting analogue research

5. Statistical significance is used to evaluate
    A. The causal relationship between variables
    B. The practical significance of research results
    C. Whether results are accurate
    D. Whether results occurred by chance

6. Which of the following "explanations" of the correlation between cigarette smoking and cancer illustrates the third-variable problem in correlational research

- A. Genetic factors cause people to have cancer and like cigarettes
- B. Having cancer causes people to enjoy the taste of cigarettes
- C. Younger people smoke cigarettes less but are more likely to use other drugs
- D. Being around people who smoke cigarettes is associated with developing cancer

7. What experimental design is illustrated by the following; A group of people are identified as all having the same psychological problem. Half receive a new therapy and their improvement is compared to the improvement of the others.

- A. Case history
- B. Correlational method
- C. Experiment
- D. Single-subject research

8. What is the dependent variable in the following study; Students in Abnormal Psychology are assigned to large lecture classes conducted either by a senior professor or by a graduate assistant. Half of them are also assigned to small discussion groups conducted by the same instructor. At the end of the semester all students take the same standardized final exam and their scores are compared.

- A. Students' motivation to study Abnormal Psychology
- B. Experience of the instructors
- C. Discussion groups (or their absence)
- D. Final exam scores

9. Analogue research is often used in studying causes of abnormality because

- A. More complex variables can be studied
- B. Inferences about causation are more easily made
- C. Other designs raise ethical problems
- D. External validity is more easily achieved

10. In single-subject research a ____________ design involves applying the same treatment to several behaviors one at a time
   A. Multiple-baseline
   B. Reversal
   C. Mixed
   D. ABAB

11. Mixed designs combine features of ____________ techniques
   A. Single-subject and correlational
   B. Correlational and experimental
   C. Analogue and reversal
   D. Case study and single-subject

SHORT ANSWER

1. A case study can have great impact on a theory if the case study (does what?) . . .

theory's predictions are proven F

2. A study of the relationship between years of driving experience and frequency of auto accidents would be likely to find a correlation coefficient between (what two numbers?) . . .

0 & -1.0

3. Give two examples of "classificatory variables".

age, sex

4. What characteristic of experimental designs makes them different from correlational designs?

ind. variable is manipulated

5. Experiments are said to be internally valid if . . .

effect attributed in ind't variable

6. Professor Jones finds that females get better scores than males on his essay tests. He would like to prove this happens because they give better answers - not because of sexual bias on his part. Describe a double-blind procedure he could use to do this.

7. What single-subject research design is illustrated by the following?
   To study the effect of diet on running, Joe records how fast he runs each day while he eats junk food or a well-balanced diet on alternating weeks.

reversal

8. In what kind of situations can reversal or ABAB designs not be used?

not ethical
not possible to go back to original site

9. Briefly describe a general limitation of all single-subject designs.

difficult to generalize results

10. Give an example of a mixed research design.

ANSWERS TO SELF-TEST, CHAPTER 5

MULTIPLE-CHOICE

1. C (p. 94)
2. D (p. 94-95)
3. A (p. 96)
4. B (p. 99)
5. D (p. 100)
6. A (p. 102)
7. C (p. 103-104)
8. D (p. 103)
9. C (p. 105)
10. A (p. 107
11. B (p. 108-109)

SHORT ANSWER

1. Provides a negative instance. That is, provides an example where the theory's predictions prove false. (p. 98-99)

2. Zero and -1.00 (assuming that more experienced drivers have fewer accidents. (p. 99-100)

3. Any dimension or classification of people based on characteristics they bring with them such as age, sex, mental status, etc. (p. 101)

4. The independent variable is actually manipulated or changed. (p. 103)

5. The effect can be confidently attributed to the independent variable. (p. 104)

6. Professor Jones could have someone else, who will not be involved in grading the tests, remove all names and identifying information from the test papers before he scores them. (. 104)

7. Reversal or ABAB design (p. 107)

8. When it is not ethically or practically possible to go back to the original behavior or state. (p. 107)

9. It is difficult to generalize the results. That is, to show that the same results would be obtained from other

individuals. (p. 106)

10. Your example should include tow independent variables, one of which is simply measured (a classificatory variable) and one of which is manipulated. For example: compare test scores of male and female students (a classificatory variable) after they spend two hours hearing a lecture or reading the text (a manipulation). (p. 108-109)

6 Anxiety Disorders

OVERVIEW

The first five chapters have discussed a number of basic ideas and issues in abnormal psychology. These concepts provide a framework for surveying the various forms of abnormality. You will want to refer back to these chapters periodically as you study the rest of the text.

Chapters 6 through 17 survey these forms of abnormality. They are divided into four major groups which, along with some examples, are:

- Part 2: Emotional Disorders and Reactions to Stress such as phobias, memory loss, and ulcers,
- Part 3: Social Problems such as anti-social individuals, alcohol and drug problems, and sexual problems,
- Part 4: Schizophrenia characterized by confused thinking and being out of contact with reality,
- Part 5: Developmental Disorders such as hyperactivity, mental retardation, and problems of the elderly.

Part 6, which is the last four chapters in the text, discusses methods of treatment as well as legal and ethical issues in treatment. Although treatments are mentioned in discussing each problem, these last chapters deal with treatment more systematically.

Now would be a good time to look over the topics of all these chapters. Notice that they cover a wide range of problem behaviors, from seemingly bizarre problems such as schizophrenia to relatively normal problems such as sexual dysfunctions. A number of them are matters of contemporary social debate, such as intelligence and retardation.

Chapters 6 thru 9 cover problems that are related to anxiety, emotions, and stress. Chapter 6 deals with Anxiety Disorders characterized directly by anxiety. Chapters 7 and 8 discuss disorders in which emotionality and stress lead to other problems. In Chapter 7 these problems are physical complaints of being blind, lame, in pain, etc. (Somatoform Disorders) or disruptions of memory, consciousness, and identity (Dissociative Disorders). In Chapter 8 they appear as physical tissue change and damage such as in ulcers and heart disease. Finally Chapter 9 discusses Affective Disorders including depression, mania, and suicide.

CHAPTER SUMMARY

Chapter 6 begins the survey by discussing Anxiety Disorders. In studying the chapter, look for the format described below (Notes to Students, #2). Three kinds of anxiety Disorders are discussed.

Phobias are relatively common disorders involving intense, unreasonable, disruptive, fears of particular situations. They include agoraphobia or fear of being away from one's home and familiar surroundings, social phobia or fear of public embarrassment, and simple phobias such as fear of snakes or of the dark. Psychoanalysts view phobias as defenses against repressed conflicts. Behaviorists have offered classical, operant, modeling, and cognitive models for the development of phobias. Physiologically oriented researchers suggest that autonomic nervous system lability (becoming physiologically aroused easily) constitutes a diathesis or predisposition for these problems.

Anxiety States consist of three problems. (1) Panic Disorders are sudden, unexpected, attacks of anxiety. Research is limited but suggests that these people escalate minor worries into full-blown panic due to physical or psychological factors. (2) People with Generalized Anxiety Disorder live in relatively constant tension. Psychoanalysts argue that their tension results from unconscious, unresolved, conflicts. Behaviorists suggest that, when examined closely, the tension can be tied to particular circumstances so that the problems are kinds of phobias. Humanists have also focused on chronic anxiety suggesting that it develops as people deny their own self-worth and accept others' critical opinions of them. (3) People with Obsessive-compulsive Disorders are bothered by unwanted thoughts (obsessions) and/or feel compelled to engage in repetitive rituals (compulsions) lest they be overcome by anxiety. Psychoanalysts propose that obsessions and compulsions reflect struggles to control id impulses which are only partly successful. Behaviorists suggest they are learned avoidance responses.

Therapies for the Anxiety States follow from views about their causes. Psychoanalysts seek to uncover the repressed conflicts. Behaviorists use a variety of techniques to reduce the anxiety and teach more effective behaviors. Humanists help people recognize their own desires and accept responsibility for their own lives. Physiological treatment using tranquilizers is common although side-effects are a problem.

Posttraumatic Stress Disorder is a new label reflecting a recognition that traumatic events such as disasters or combat may effect anyone. Traumas may produce aftereffects including anxiety, a numbing feeling of being separate from others, and intrusive vivid memories. Although the disorder existed in earlier wars, recent interest has focused on the Vietnam War where both combat conditions and anti-war sentiment at home were stressful. For Vietnam veterans treatment has focused on self-help "rap groups".

NOTES TO STUDENTS

1. This is a good time to warn you of a common experience among students studying abnormal psychology. Often, students in these courses come to believe they have the problem covered in each chapter. For example, you may think you have an anxiety disorder when studying Chapter 6, depression in Chapter 9, and schizophrenia in Chapter 14. If this happens to you, don't be surprised. The various problems covered in the text are probably exaggerations of very normal tendencies in all of us. If you can see tendencies in yourself, it probably means you have developed a meaningful understanding of the problem. Of course, if you are seriously concerned, you can discuss the matter with your instructor or someone at your school's counseling center. They are used to such situations and you may be surprised at how easily they understand your concerns.

2. As you study these chapters you will discover that each follows the same general outline. First, the problem is defined and any issues regarding it's classification in DSM-III are discussed. Second, theories and research into its causes are described. Typically this description includes the Psychoanalytic, Behavioral, and Physiological paradigms. Finally, various treatments are summarized under the same three paradigms. Of course the outline varies but you will find it helpful to look for this kind of outline as you study each chapter and to organize your study notes around it.

STUDY OBJECTIVES

After studying Chapter 6 you should know

1. That the term neurosis is based on the psychoanalytic idea that anxiety is caused by unconscious conflict, and some psychopathologists believe it should be replaced by more descriptive terms.

2. That phobias, anxiety states, and posttraumatic stress are the major categories of anxiety disorders listed in DSM-III.

3. That a phobia is a disrupting, fear-mediated avoidance, out of proportion to the actual danger of the particular object or situation that is feared. Some phobias are more disruptive than others.

4. Psychoanalytic theory focuses on the content of phobias -- their symbolic meaning, while learning theory focuses on their function -- the avoidance of a feared situation.

5. That behavior genetics is the study of individual differences in behavior that are attributable in part to differences in genetic makeup.

6. That panic disorder, generalized anxiety disorder, and obsessive-compulsive disorder are the subcategories of the anxiety states.

7. That a cognitive behavioral view holds that the experience of helplessness and lack of control is a major cause of anxiety.

8. That Posttraumatic stress disorder, found in many Vietnam veterans, is a new diagnostic category in DSM-III that refers to the after effects of the experience of disaster.

9. That,although the treatment of the various anxiety disorders generally follows from basic theoretical assumptions, more and more therapists of different theoretical orientations emphasize active interventions such as the need to confront the feared situation or to prevent ritualistic behavior.

KEY TERMS

Neuroses (p. 114) group of nonpsychotic disorders characterized by unrealistic anxiety

Anxiety Disorder (p. 115) Phobia
Anxiety states
Panic disorder

Phobia (p. 115) unrealistic fear

Agoraphobia (p. 117) fear of public places ~ unable to escape
often begins w/ panic attacks

Social phobia (p. 117) persistent fear (irrational) linked to the presence of others > women
adolescence

Simple phobia (p. 118)

not an adq. model → Vicarious conditioning (p. 120) learning of phobic reactions by observing others
extinguishes quickly

Autonomic lability (p. 124) the extent to which the autonomic nervous s. is involved in fear → behavior
(genetically determined)

Systematic desensitization (p. 127) BEHAVIORAL
imagines frightful scenes while in state of relaxation

Flooding (p. 127) forces exposure at full intensity

Panic Disorder (p. 128)

Depersonalization (p. 128) feelings of being outside of one's body

Derealization (p. 128)

Generalized anxiety Disorder (p. 129)

Helplessness (p. 130)

Gestalt therapy (p. 133)

Obsessive-compulsive Disorder (p. 134)

Obsession (p. 134)

Compulsion (p. 134)

Posttraumatic Stress Disorder (p. 138)

STUDY QUESTIONS

1. Define "Neuroses" pointing out the theoretical assumptions involved. How has DSM-III dealt with this term? (p. 114)

PHOBIAS (P. 115 - 128)

2. What are phobias and why have psychologists disagreed on sub-classifying them? Identify three subcatagories of phobias. (p. 115 - 118)

3. Summarize one Freudian and three behavioral theories of phobias with the criticisms of each (p. 118 - 120)

4. Summarize Ellis' behavioral cognitive view of social anxiety. (p. 120 - 121)

5. What physiological factor might predispose a person to develop phobias (or other anxiety disorders)? (p. 122 - 124) Summarize and critique the genetic studies supporting this possibility. (p. 124 - 126)

6. Summarize the psychoanalytic and three behavioral approaches to therapy for phobias. What do all these techniques have in common? What is the principal problem with the common somatic treatment? (p. 126 - 128)

ANXIETY STATES (p. 128 - 138)

7. Describe the characteristics of panic attacks. How much do we know about them? (p. 128 - 129)

8. Summarize the characteristics of Generalized Anxiety Disorders. (p. 129)

9. Briefly summarize five views on the cause of generalized anxiety. (p. 129 - 132) Summarize the treatment approach which has grown out of each (plus the community approach). (p. 132 - 134)

   (You will find it helpful to compare these views to the views on phobias.)

10. Define and give several examples of obsessions and compulsions. How are these definitions different from way we commonly use the terms? (p. 134 - 136)

11. Briefly summarize four theories of Obsessive-compulsive Disorders (One psychoanalytic, two behavioral, and one cognitive). (p. 136 - 137)

12. Briefly summarize four treatments for Obsessive-compulsive Disorders (One psychoanlytic, two behavioral, and one physiological). How effective are these? (p. 137 - 138)

POSTTRAUMATIC STRESS DISORDER (P. 138 - 143)

13. What are the characteristics of Posttraumatic stress disorder? How is this disorder different from the others in the chapter? (p. 138 - 139)

14. In the Vietnam War what combat and social stresses existed? How have professionals (especially in the Veterans Administration) and veterans themselves dealt with the problem? (p. 139 - 143)

SELF-TEST, CHAPTER 6

MULTIPLE-CHOICE

1. As compared to other psychological problems, phobias are relatively,
   A. Common and mildly disabling
   B. Uncommon and mildly disabling
   C. Common and strongly disabling
   D. Uncommon and strongly disabling

2. ____________ is an unreasonable fear of leaving home and of being in crowds or open, exposed places.
   A. Simple phobia
   B. Agoraphobia
   C. Social phobia
   D. Claustrophobia

3. In the psychoanalytic view, phobias develop when repressed conflicts
   A. Reappear in exaggerated form
   B. Reawaken childhood Oedipal fears
   C. Break through into conscious awareness of the original conflict
   D. Are displaced to a symbolically related situation

4. ____________ suggests that phobias develop when a neutral stimulus is paired with a traumatic event so that escaping or avoiding the stimulus becomes reinforcing.
   A. Ellis' cognitive theory
   B. The diathesis-stress theory
   C. The avoidance conditioning model
   D. Freudian theory

5. The modeling or vicarious conditioning approach suggests that an unreasonable fear of snakes could develop in individuals
   A. Whose parents are afraid of snakes
   B. Who are bitten by a snake
   C. For whom snakes are, unconsciously, sexually symbolic
   D. That grow up in regions where snakes are common

6. Autonomic nervous system arouse-ability or lability
   A. Has been suggested as a factor in compulsive behavior
   B. Was extensively studied by John Watson
   C. Influences how well people respond to the empty-chair technique
   D. May be a diathesis in phobias

7. Which therapy approach argues that one should NOT try to directly deal with or eliminate a phobia?
   A. Psychoanalysis
   B. Systematic desensitization
   C. Flooding
   D. Somatic

8. Treatment of phobias with tranquilizers
   A. Has not generally be successful
   B. Can lead to drug dependency
   C. Is done only in unusual circumstances
   D. Has become the treatment of choice among psychologists

9. Which of the following disorders is least understood?
   A. Phobia
   B. Panic Disorder
   C. Generalized Anxiety Disorder
   D. Obsessive-compulsive Disorder

10. According to psychoanalysis the difference between phobias and generalized anxiety is that, with generalized anxiety, the repressed conflict
   A. Developed earlier in childhood
   B. Is between the ego and super-ego
   C. Is not allowed even indirect expression
   D. Involves hostile-aggressive urges

11. Which of the following is NOT an obsession?
   A. Persistent fear of not locking the door
   B. Persistent urge to make barking noises
   C. Persistent doubts that the door has been locked
   D. Persistent checking for one's keys

12. The text argues that Vietnam soldiers experienced increased stress because
   A. They were more constantly in combat
   B. They were less psychologically prepared for combat
   C. Many at home saw little value in their efforts
   D. Many had good jobs waiting them at home

SHORT ANSWER

1. What assumption was the basis for the term "neuroses"?
Freudian

2. Define "social phobia". unreasonable fear of public situations

3. List three theoretical possibilities which have been considered in research on social anxiety.
(3) irrational beliefs must be approved (1) unfortunate episode that classically cond. the ind. (2) lack of social skills (hasn't learned to behave w/others

4. Describe what is done in systematic desensitization as a treatment for phobias. people imagine themselves in the feared situation

5. In what way are panic disorder and generalized anxiety disorder similar? patients are chronically anxious
not linked to a specific situation

6. What is the basis for generalized anxiety according to cognitive-behavioral views? the person is not in control

7. Summarize humanistic views on the cause of anxiety.
patients are preoccupied w/ 2 conflicting self concepts
accept neg opinions held by others interfering w self-enhancing image

8. Humanistic treatment of anxiety seeks to help the person (do what?).
realize that they aren't going to be accepted w/ all (rely on their own desires, urges)

9. According to psychoanalysis, what is the basis for obsessive, compulsive behaviors?
struggle betw'n id + defense mechanisms
fixed at anal stage
Defense mechanisms attempt to control unacceptable desires

ANSWERS TO SELF-TEST, CHAPTER 6

MULTIPLE-CHOICE

1. A (p. 115)	2. B (p. 117)	3. D (p. 119)
4. C (p. 119)	5. A (p. 120)	6. D (p. 122-124)
7. A (p. 126)	8. B (p. 128)	9. B (p. 128)
10. C (p. 129)	11. D (p. 134)	12. C (p. 141)

SHORT ANSWER

1. Freudian assumption that many problems were based, directly or indirectly, on repressed anxiety. (p. 114)

2. Unreasonable fear of public scrutiny or embarrassment. (As distinguished from agorophobia or fear of public, unfamiliar situations.) (p. 117)

3. 1) Unfortunate social experiences, 2) lack of social skills, 3) irrational beliefs - such as "It's awful if someone does not approve of me." (p. 120-121)

4. Individual is taught how to relax deeply. Then, while relaxed, person experiences (perhaps, by imagining them) a series of gradually more fearful situations. (p. 127)

5. Person experiences anxiety which is not linked to a particular situation. (p. 128-129)

6. Helplessness or lack of control over events. (p. 131-132)

7. Anxiety develops as we accept others negative opinions rather than our own natural, positive, opinions of ourselves. (p. 132-133)

8. Become more aware of, trust, and express their own feelings, urges, desires. (p. 132-134)

9. They are defense mechanisms or partially successful attempts to control unacceptable, repressed desires. (p. 136-137)

7 Somatoform and Dissociative Disorders

OVERVIEW

Chapter 7 is the second of four chapters on emotional disorders and reactions to stress. The previous chapter discussed disorders involving fairly direct struggles with anxiety. These included chronic anxiety, phobias or unreasonable fears, and obsessions and compulsions in which people think and do things in order to control anxiety.

Chapters 7 and 8 describe disorders in which people may not directly complain of anxiety but have other problems that appear related to anxiety and stress in some way. In Chapter 8 the other problems involve physical damage and tissue change such as an ulcer (Psychophysiological Disorders). In Chapter 7 the other problems are physical complaints such as complaints of pain or inability to walk (Somatoform Disorders) or are problems of memory, consciousness, and identity such as amnesia (Dissociative Disorders).

Chapter 9 concludes this part of the text by discussing disorders of affect involving feelings such as depression. Then a new part of the text begins which covers social problems including criminality, drug abuse, and sexual problems.

CHAPTER SUMMARY

Chapter 7 covers two groups of disorders in which there is a loss of functioning with no physical basis. The symptoms seem to serve a psychological purpose.

Somatoform Disorders are characterized by physical complaints which have no physiological basis. They include two disorders. In Conversion Disorders there is a loss of sensory or motor functioning. For example; a loss of vision, touch, etc. or of the ability to walk, talk, etc. In Somatization Disorder there are multiple physical complaints (headaches, various pains, fatigue, etc) involving repeated visits to physicians and medical treatment.

Theories of somatoform disorders deal primarily with conversions and remain speculative. Conversion disorders have been a central focus of psychoanalysis which proposes that repressed impulses are "converted" into the physical symptoms and seeks to uncover the impulses. Behavioral theorists suggest that people are reinforced for being in the role of a "sick" person and seek to reduce anxiety while teaching more socially effective behaviors. Sociocultural, genetic, and physiological speculations have been offered.

Dissociative Disorders are disorders of awareness and memory. In psychogenic amnesia the individual is unable to recall important personal information; often of traumatic events. Psychogenic fugue involves a more encompassing memory loss in which the person leaves home and assumes a new identity. In Multiple personality two or more separate and distinct personalities occur in alternation, each having it's own memories, behaviors, and life styles.

Psychoanalysis suggests that dissociative disorders reflect a massive repression of memory or identity that protects the individual when repressed conflicts have broken through into awareness. Similarly, behavioral theory describes dissociative disorders as avoidance responses motivated by anxiety. Thus both propose that treatment focus on the anxiety that presumably provoked the problem.

STUDY OBJECTIVES

After studying Chapter 7 you should know

1. That conversion disorder and somatization disorder are the two major categories of somatoform disorders. 

2. That, in conversion disorders, there is no apparent organic difficulty, but the operations of the musculature or sensory functions are impaired making the symptoms seem to be linked with psychological factors.

3. That it is difficult to distinguish conversion disorders from physical illnesses or from malingering.

4. That somatization disorder is characterized by recurrent, multiple somatic complaints for which medical attention is sought but which have no apparent physical basis.

5. That conversion disorders occupy a central place in psychoanalytic thinking because their nature leads one to consider the concept of the unconscious.

6. That while Freud allowed for secondary gain or direct reinforcement for the symptoms of a conversion disorder, he suggested that the primary gain was avoidance of represssed id impulses.

7. That while evidence from experimental psychology supports the notion that many processes are unconscious, there is no support for the existence of "the unconscious".

8. That the dissociative disorders include psychogenic amnesia, psychogenic fugue, and multiple personality.

9. That the dissociative disorders suggest the plausibility of Freud's concept of repression.

10. That little is known about the relative efficacy of treatments for either somatoform or dissociative disorders.

KEY TERMS

Somatoform disorder (p. 146) physical symptoms suggest a physical prob. have no phsiological cause

Psychogenic pain disorder (p. 146) person reports severe, long-lasting pain that can't be accounted for by organic pathology

Hypocondriasis (p. 146) person is preoccupied w/ fears of having a serious disease

Conversion disorder (p. 146) operations of musculature or sensory functions are impaired, but the neuromuscular apparatus & body organs are sound

Hysteria (p. 146) physical incapacity or paralysis is not due to a physiological dysfunction

Malingering (p. 148) faking an incapacity in order to avoid a responsibility

La belle indifference (p. 148) relative lack of concern

Briquet's syndrome Somatization disorder (p. 148) recurrent, multiple somatic complaints which have no physical cause late adolescence (common in ♀)

Social-skills training (p. 155) Behavioral teaching effective ways to approach & talk w/people keep eye contact (means of relating to others)

Dissociative disorder (p. 156) normal integration of consciousness, memory, or identity is suddenly or temp. altered

Psychogenic amnesia (p. 157) person can't recall personal info after a stressful episode

Psychogenic fugue (p. 157) totally amnesic - moves away & assumes new identity

Multiple personality (p. 157) at least 2 personalities each has own memories, relationships, & behavior patterns

STUDY QUESTIONS

SOMATOFORM DISORDERS (p. 146 - 156)

1. Describe four types of somatoform disorders. (Two of the four are not discussed further.) What do all four types have in common? (p. 146)

Conversion Disorder
Somatization Disorder
Psychogenic pain disorder
hypochondriasis

2. Give some examples of conversion symptoms involving loss of (a) muscular activity and (b) sensory input. Describe two problems in diagnosing conversions. (p. 146 - 148)

① true neurological probs may be misdiagnosed as conversion disorders

② symptoms labeled as conversion reactions thought to have psychological causes may be physical disorders

3. Describe the somatic complaints and related behaviors which distinguish somatization disorder. (p. 148 - 150)

headaches, fatigue, allergies, chest pains, etc.

4. How did the study of conversion disorders lead Freud to important concepts? Summarize Freud's theory of conversions including his later refinement of it. (p. 150 - 151)

led to opportunity to invoke concept of unconscious

specific conversion symptoms related to trauma that caused them

- Disorders rooted in early unresolved Electra complex

primary gain; avoidance of previously repressed id impulses

secondary gain; allows the escape from current unpleasant life sit.

5. How and why have some contemporary psychoanalysts revised Freud's theory? (p. 151 - 153)

see problem originating during the oral period during the formation of the infants basic security system

6. Describe three other theories of conversion disorders. How well is each supported by research? (p. 153 - 155)

sociocultural theories: decrease in conversion disorders due to the general relaxing of sexual mores

behavioral: person attempts to behave according to his own conception of how a person with a disease affecting the motor or sensory abilities would act

genetic + physiological:

7. Why has little research been done on the psychological treatment of somatoform disorders? What is the aim of psychoanalysis and behavioral therapy in treating these disorders? (p. 155 - 156)

DISSOCIATIVE DISORDERS (p. 156 - 163)

8. Define and distinguish among three major dissociative disorders (p. 156 - 160). Distinguish between multiple personality and "split personality" as the term is used to describe schizophrenia. (See footnote, p. 158)

psychogenic amnesia
psychogenic fugue
mult. personality

9. Summarize the psychoanalytic and learning theory views of dissociative disorders. (p. 160 - 162)

10. Describe the traditional therapeutic approach to treating dissociative disorders. Why is hypnosis often used and how effective is it? (p. 162 - 163)

SELF-TEST, CHAPTER 7

MULTIPLE-CHOICE

1. The common characteristic of all somatoform disorders is
   A. Pain
   B. Anxiety
   C. Physical symptoms
   D. Hearing voices

2. Which of the following terms is least like the others?
   A. Conversion disorder
   B. Somatization disorder
   C. Psychogenic pain disorder
   D. Hypochondriasis
   E. Amnesia

3. In order to distinguish between a conversion disorder and malingering, it would be most useful to know,
   A. Whether the individual is eager to discuss their problem
   B. Whether the complaint makes sense anatomically
   C. Whether the individual has a history of violent behavior
   D. The individual's age, sex, and socio-economic level

4. Researchers studying somatoform disorders in which people claim to be blind have shown that
   A. Visual stimuli do not reach the brain
   B. Visual stimuli are blocked from awareness
   C. Visual stimuli do not effect behavior
   D. The people are malingering

5. Psychoanalytic treatment for conversion disorders seeks to help the client,
   A. Realize that their problem is psychological in nature
   B. Uncover the conflict they have presumably repressed
   C. Become more relaxed in the presence of the feared stimulus
   D. Learn to control their often violent and aggressive urges

6. Behavioral treatments for somatoform disorders seek to
   A. Reduce anxiety levels using systematic desensitization
   B. Eliminate the problem behaviors using punishment
   C. Uncover repressed conflicts using hypnosis
   D. Teach more socially appropriate techniques for interacting with others

7. The distinction between psychogenic amnesia and fugue is
   A. Whether the persons' actions are purposeful
   B. Whether the person is able to talk and reason
   C. Whether the person assumes a new identity elsewhere
   D. Whether the problem follows a severely stressful event
   E. The length of time the problem continues

8. Multiple personality can be loosely described as being like
   A. Two different people in the same body
   B. A person not knowing what they are doing
   C. Forgetting who you are and where you have been
   D. A split personality

9. All theories of Dissociative disorders view these problems as
   A. Breakdowns in the body's coping systems
   B. Relatively deliberate, conscious, attempts to avoid situations
   C. The result of childhood conflicts that are unresolved
   D. Methods of protecting the individual from stress

10. The preferred behavioral method of treating dissociative disorders is
   A. Systematic desensitization
   B. Social skills training
   C. Similar to psychoanalytic methods
   D. None of the above - behavioral methods are not effective

SHORT ANSWER

1. Individuals with somatization disorder have many and varied physical complaints which have no apparent physical basis.

2. Identify two problems in diagnosing conversion disorders.

physical probs
malingering

3. Psychoanalytic theories suggest that somatoform disorders result from . . .

conflicts converted to a physical form

4. Summarize a behavioral account of the cause of conversion disorders.

patient acts how they think a sick person would act

5. Sociocultural theories suggest that conversion reactions develop under what conditions?

encourage physical expressions of anxiety

6. Why is little known regarding the effectiveness of psychological treatments for somatoform disorders?

people seek medical help

7. According to psychoanalysis, what kind of event triggers dissociative reactions?

8. Research on state-dependent memory may help explain dissociative disorders by showing that . . .

9. There has been little research on dissociative disorders because . . .

states are rare

10. Dissociative disorders (more than other disorders) are commonly treated by psychoanalytic methods because . . .

ANSWERS TO SELF-TEST, CHAPTER 7

MULTIPLE-CHOICE

1. C (p. 146))
2. E (p. 146&156)
3. A (p. 148)
4. B (p. 151)
5. B (p. 155)
6. D (p. 155)
7. C (p. 157)
8. A (p. 157-158)
9. D (p. 160)
10. C (p. 163)

SHORT ANSWER

1. Somatization disorder (Briquet's syndrome) (p. 148)

2. Distinguishing conversion disorders from 1) physical problems and 2) malingering (p. 147-148)

3. Psychological conflicts which are transformed, distorted, or converted into physical form. (p. 150-151)

4. The individual is acting as he/she believes sick people should act. (p. 154)

5. When social codes tolerate or encourage physical, rather than psychological, expressions of anxiety. (p. 153)

6. Because such individuals seek medical rather than psychological treatment. (p. 155-156)

7. Repressed conflicts break through into awareness and the person can only "forget" what happened by repressing the entire memory. (p. 160)

8. People do not remember as well when in a different emotional state. (p. 161)

9. These states are rare. (p. 161-163)

10. Psychoanalytic concepts such as unconscious and repression clearly seem applicable. (p. 162)

8 Psychophysiological Disorders

OVERVIEW

This is the third of four chapters on emotional disorders involving stress, worry, and feelings.

The last two chapters have covered psychological disorders that are linked to anxiety. The disorders in Chapter 6 included chronic anxiety, unreasonable fears or phobias, and recurrent thoughts or actions (obsessions and compulsions) which protect the individual from anxiety. Chapter 7 covered two groups of disorders. Dissociative Disorders involve problems in memory, consciousness, and identity in which the individuals dissociate or psychologically separate themselves from stressful experiences. Somatoform Disorders involved stress expressed in physical symptoms including pain, fatigue, and sensorimotor symptoms such as inability to see or walk.

It should, by now, be clear that anxiety is common and is a source of much psychological suffering. In addition to its psychological effects, anxiety can also have physical effects. While symptoms of the disorders in Chapter 7 may mimic physical problems, they do not involve physical tissue damage and change. The symptoms may include inability to remember events or to see but no nerve damage or other physical changes account for the problem. The Psychophysiological Disorders in Chapter 8 do involve physical tissue damage and change. Ulcers and heart attacks are examples of these disorders.

After Chapter 8 the next chapter discusses emotional disorders involving affect or feelings; primarily depression. The text then begins Part 3 which deals with Social Problems. Social problems are not commonly considered disorders or "illnesses" but are of concern to society and/or to the individuals with the problems. Examples of these problems include criminality, substance abuse, and a variety of sexual problems ranging from rape to voyeurism ("Peeping Toms") to impotence.

CHAPTER SUMMARY

Probably all physical illnesses involve psychological stress to some degree. Chapter 8 focuses on those physical problems where the involvement has, traditionally, been considered especially strong. The chapter discusses these Psychophysiological Disorders in general and then discusses some common examples in more detail. Generally a Diathesis-stress model accounts for these disorders by suggesting that physiological sensitivities and psychological backgrounds sensitize individuals to develop the problems when they experience particular kinds of stress.

Stress and Illness reviews research on stress and it's relation to physical illness.

Theories of Psychophysiological Disorders: An Overview identifies a number of both physiological and psychological theories leading to a multifactorial view that many factors may be involved.

Ulcers are gastrointestinal lesions which have been linked to both psychological stress and uncertainty and to physiological differences in how readily the stomach secretes fluids under stress.

Cardiovascular Disorders including hypertension and heart disease appear related to specific styles of responding to stress as well as to physiological factors.

Asthma attacks involving difficulty in breathing result from different combinations of factors including allergies and infections, psychological factors, and physiological predispositions.

Therapies for Psychophysiological Disorders include both medical treatment of the physical symptoms and psychological methods of controlling the underlying stress. Behavioral medicine, a new specialization, is developing techniques such as biofeedback to treat Psychophysiological Disorders.

STUDY OBJECTIVES

After studying Chapter 8 you should know

1. That psychophysiological disorders are distinct from conversion reactions in that they are actual physical changes that are caused or can be worsened by emotional factors.

2. That there is no listing of psychophysiological disorders in DSM III because virtually all physical illnesses are now viewed as potentially related to psychological stress.

3. That the relation found between stress and illness is far from perfect and this may be attributable to problems in measuring stress, measuring illness, or to intervening variables such as hardiness.

4. About the various theories of the link between stress and illness.

5. That, consistent with specific-reaction theory, individuals who develop ulcers appear to be predisposed to react to stress with excessive gastric secretions.

6. That holding anger in and and other Type A behaviors are related to an increased risk for high blood pressure and coronary heart disease, respectively.

7. That psychological factors are not the cause of most asthma although parent-child relationships appear to play a role in onset and maintenance of asthma.

8. That many therapists agree that reducing anxiety is the best way to alleviate the suffering from psychological disorders.

9. That behavioral medicine is a new area of psychological specialization in which psychologists work very closely with physicians in helping to alleviate physical disorders through psychological treatments.

10. That the diathesis-stress model seems to work well as a means of conceptualizing psychophysiological disorders.

KEY TERMS

Psychophysiological Disorders (p. 166) genuine physical symptoms caused or worsened by emotional factors

Psychosomatic (p. 166) psyche or mind is having an untoward effect on the body

Dualism (p. 166) deeply ingrained paradigm of human thought; humans are mental & physical; seperate but interacting

Social Readjustment Rating Scale (SRRS) (P. 168) measure life stress check off life events that have been experienced during the time period

Hardiness (p. 170) constellation of 3 clinical personality characteristics commitment, control, & challenge (easily commit themselves) believe that they can at least partially control events

Somatic-weakness theory (p. 171) the connection betw'n stress & a particular psychophysiological disorder is the weakness in a specific bodily organ asthma – emotional state

Specific reaction theory (p. 171) Ind. develops a given physchophysiological disorder because of innate tendency of the autonomic system to respond in a part. way to stress

Evolution theory (p. 171)

Multifactorial theory (p. 173) several stressors influencing in a complex fashion in the development + maintenance of a problem

Ulcers (p. 174)

Pepsinogen (p. 176) secreted by peptic cells of the gastric glands in the stomach - converted to pepsin; implicated in form. of ulcers high levels seem to be inherited

Cardiovascular disorders (p. 176)

Essential hypertension (p. 176) hypertension without an evident organic cause

Angina pectoris (p. 180) periodic chest pains (left shoulder + arm) precipitated by physical or emotional exertion + is treated by rest + medication

Myocardial infarction (p. 180) insufficient O_2 to heart not necessarily caused by exertion

Type A behavior (p. 180) overachievers, workaholics

Asthma (p. 183)

Behavioral medicine (p. 189) psychological probs linked to physical probs.

Biofeedback (p. 189) prompt info; exact info on heart rate, blood pressure, brain waves, etc.

STUDY QUESTIONS

1. Distinguish between Conversion Disorders (in Chapter 7), Psychophysiological Disorders, and physical illnesses in general. How does dualistic thinking make it difficult to understand Psychophysiological Disorders. (p. 166 - 167)

STRESS AND ILLNESS (p. 167 - 171)

2. How is the Social Readjustment Rating Scale (SRRS) used to study the relation between stress and illness? Identify two problems with the SRRS. (p. 168 - 170)

3. What is the relationship between stress and physical illnesses in general? Describe this in terms of the immune system and of hardiness (p. 170 - 171)

THEORIES OF PSYCHOPHYSIOLOGICAL DISORDERS (p. 171 - 174)

4. Briefly summarize five theories of psychophysiological disorders. How might a multifactorial theory integrate these views? (p. 171 - 174)

ULCER (p. 174 - 176)

5. What is the common characteristic of stressors that lead to ulcers? What evidence suggests a genetic and physiological predisposition to ulcers? (p. 175-176

CARDIOVASCULAR DISORDERS (p. 176 - 183)

6. Define essential hypertension and coronary heart disease. How important are these problems? (p. 176 & 179 - 180)

7. What kind of situations and responses produce short term increases in blood pressure? Why is it difficult to study long-term increases? (p. 177 - 179)

8. Summarize the research into predisposing factors by explaining, what has been found in animals, what has been found in humans, and why the human research is limited. (p. 179)

9. What is the Type A behavior pattern? How is it related to heart disease on a physical and on a psychological level? (p. 180 - 183)

ASTHMA (p. 183 - 188)

10. Describe what happens in an asthma attack. (p. 183 - 185)

11. Explain the general debate concerning the etiology of asthma? Can psychological factors produce asthma attacks? (p. 185 - 186)

12. What has been learned about the following possible contributors to asthma: Classical conditioning, the role of the family, personality, physiological predispositions? (p. 186 - 188)

THERAPIES FOR PSYCHOPHYSIOLOGICAL DISORDERS (p. 188 - 192)

13. In general what kind of treatment is needed for psychophysiological disorders? (p. 188 - 189)

14. What is "behavioral medicine"? Give some examples of how these specialists treat psychophysiological disorders. (p. 189 - 192)

SELF-TEST, CHAPTER 8

MULTIPLE-CHOICE

1. Dualism may complicate our thinking about Psychophysiological Disorders because it suggests that
   - A. Both physical and psychological factors are involved
   - B. Mind and body operate independently
   - C. These disorders must be understood at both theory and research levels
   - D. A Diathesis-stress model is needed

2. The Social Readjustment Rating Scale is used to measure
   - A. Stressfulness of recent events
   - B. Social desirability of stressful adjustments
   - C. Readjustment following recent illnesses
   - D. Effects of social prejudice on patients

3. Research suggests that individuals who get involved in what they are doing, believe they can control events, and feel challenged rather than threatened by change are prone to develop
   - A. Ulcers
   - B. Cardiovascular diseases
   - C. Asthma
   - D. None of the above - these individuals tolerate stress well

4. The ____________ theory proposes that psychophysiological disorders result because the human body is not designed to respond effectively to complex social stresses.
   - A. Somatic-weakness
   - B. Specific-reaction
   - C. Evolution
   - D. Multifactorial

5. What kind of stress seems most likely to produce ulcers according to research?
   A. Stress produced by strong desires for achievement
   B. Stress where the person has limited control
   C. Stress involving interpersonal conflicts
   D. Stress which occurs at the same time every day

6. Myocardial infarction is the technical term for
   A. High blood pressure
   B. Heart pains
   C. Heart attack
   D. High sodium cholesterol

7. Type A individuals can be described as
   A. Defeated, angry, frustrated
   B. Committed, feeling in control, enjoying challenge
   C. Personable, responsible, outgoing
   D. Achievement oriented, competitive, impatient

8. ____________ results from a variety of factors whose importance varies from individual to individual
   A. Ulcers
   B. Essential Hypertension
   C. Cardiovascular disease
   D. Asthma

9. Which of the following is LEAST important in the development of asthma according to research
   A. Allergies
   B. Respiratory infections
   C. Classical conditioning
   D. Parent-child interactions

10. A major problem in treating individuals with Type A behavior patterns is that
   A. Society encourages Type A behavior
   B. Treatment is costly and time-consuming
   C. The pattern is difficult to detect early
   D. Type B patterns are a common side-effect

SHORT ANSWER

1. Psychophysiological disorders are not a catagory in DSM-III because . . .

2. Describe the possible physiological link between stress and illness. Immune system functions poorly under stress

3. Summarize the somatic-weakness theory.
what ever is weakest will be affected under stress

4. According to the specific reaction theory psychophysiological disorders result from differences in the way particular individuals respond physically to stress.

5. How does psychoanalysis account for the fact that people develop different psychophysiological disorders when exposed to the (apparently) same stressors? unconscious conflicts influence how people respond to stress - diff. disorders

6. What physiological factor may predispose some people to develop ulcers under stress? pepsinogen

7. Define "essential hypertension".
no organic cause ~ high blood pressure

8. According to research blood pressure may remain low in individuals who respond to stress by . . .
reacting assertively

9. Summarize the results of research on the role of the family in causing asthma.

10. Define "behavioral medicine".

ANSWERS TO SELF-TEST, CHAPTER 8

MULTIPLE-CHOICE

1. B (p. 166)
2. A (p. 168)
3. D (p. 170-171)
4. C (p. 171-172)
5. B (p. 175)
6. C (p. 179)
7. D (p. 181)
8. D (p. 185)
9. C (p. 186)
10. A (p. 192)

SHORT ANSWER

1. Virtually all physical diseases are potentially related to psychological stress (p. 167)

2. Immune system which protects body from physical illness appears to function poorly under stress. (p. 170)

3. Disorders will appear in whichever physical system is weakest or most vulnerable to stress. (p. 171)

4. Specific-reaction (p. 171)

5. Unconscious, unresolved, conflicts influence how individuals respond to stress thus producing different disorders. (p. 172)

6. High pepsinogen secretions in the stomach (p. 176)

7. High blood pressure with no obvious organic cause. (p. 176-177)

8. Reacting assertively. Expressing anger in effective, socially acceptable ways. (p. 178-179)

9. Results are confusing. Some studies show no relation. Others studies find disturbed relationships in some asthmatics, however these could be the cause or result of asthma. (p. 187)

10. A branch of behavior therapy that deals with psychological factors in physical illness. (p. 189)

9 Affective Disorders

OVERVIEW

The previous three chapters have covered a wide range of problems related in one way or another to anxiety and stress. Chapter 9 will cover another group of emotionally based disorders - the Affective Disorders.

So far Chapter 6 has shown that anxiety and stress can lead fairly directly to Anxiety Disorders. Chapter 7 showed they can also lead to symptoms involving sensory and motor loses (Somatoform Disorders) or involving problems in memory, consciousness, and identity (Dissociative Disorders). Anxiety and stress can also produce physical damage and illness, especially in Psychophysiological Disorders covered in Chapter 8.

Chapter 9 turns to Affective Disorders; that is disorders of mood or feelings. By far the most common affective disorder involves a lowered mood or depression. Some people also experience a heightened mood of elation or mania. Such people usually swing back and forth between mania and depression. Such a disorder is called "bipolar".

Like anxiety, sadness and elation are normal experiences for most people from time to time. However, when they become a dominant force in people's lives, they constitute a psychological disorder.

Chapter 9 concludes the text's examination of disorders that are primarily emotional in nature. The next four chapters will be devoted to Social Problems characterized by behaviors or personality traits that are of concern either to society or to the affected individual. Examples of such problems include criminality, drug abuse, sexual disorders such as rape and incest, and sexual dysfunctions such as impotence and frigidity.

CHAPTER SUMMARY

As reflected in the DSM-III categories, clinicians find that depression may occur alone (unipolar) or may alternate with mania (bipolar). In addition common practice and DSM-III recognize a difference between major disorders and less serious but chronic disorders. In order to avoid confusion the chapter begins by describing General Characteristics of Depression and Mania. It then goes on to present the Formal Diagnostic Listings in DSM-III. This approach is slightly different from previous chapters.

Psychological Theories of Depression all propose that depression reflects difficulty in adjusting to loss. Psychoanalytic theory suggests that dependent people remain stuck in sadness because they cannot work through the anger which people also experience following a loss. Beck's cognitive theory suggests that depressives illogically blame themselves for any negative events and Seligman suggests that this results from early helplessness in controlling negative events. Learning theorists have compared depression to the extinction of behavior following loss of reinforcement.

Psychological Theories of Bipolar Disorder are not well developed. Generally theorists have utilized theories of depression by proposing that mania protects individuals from experiencing their depression.

Physiological Theories of Affective Disorders indicate a genetic predisposition, especially for bipolar disorders, and suggest that both mania and depression reflect differences in the supply of particular neurotransmitters - chemicals that carry messages between neurons in the brain.

Therapy for Affective Disorders includes psychotherapeutic approaches derived from psychological theories of the causes of depression as well as electroconvulsive shock and antidepressant drugs.

Suicide is partially related to depression although many suicidal individuals are not obviously depressed or otherwise disordered. Suicide facts and myths are reviewed suggesting that existing theories have difficulty accounting for the many causes of suicide. Suicide prevention centers exist in most communities to help people overcome self-destructive urges.

STUDY OBJECTIVES

After studying Chapter 9 you should know

1. That the two major affective disorders listed in DSM III are major depression and bipolar disorder.

2. That Freud viewed depression as resulting from a complex process including fixation at the oral stage, real or symbolic loss, and incomplete mourning work. His theories have conceptual problems, however.

3. That Aaron Beck suggests that depression results from making certain logical errors and argues that depressives have a negative self-schema.

4. That Martin Seligman's theory of depression suggests that learned helplessness, the cause of depression, is a consequence of experiencing a failure to control events in your life and attributing this failure to internal, global stable causes.

5. That learning theorists argue that depression results from a reduction in reinforcement.

6. That there are very few psychological theories of mania but those that exist propose that mania is a defense against depression.

7. That genetic data indicate there is a heritable component to both bipolar disorder and major depression, although evidence indicates genetics is more prominent in bipolar disorder.

8. That biochemical theories of depression indicate that a depletion of certain neurotransmitters, particularly norepinephrine and serotonin, may underline the psychic state of depression.

9. That biochemical and psychological theories of depression are not necessarily incompatible but may explain the same phenomenon at different levels of analysis.

10. That empirical work indicates that Beck's cognitive theory appears to be the most effective psychological treatment for depression, and, in fact, may be superior to medication.

11. That there are a number of effective somatic treatments for depression including electroconvulsive therapy and antidepressant drugs. Lithium is a useful drug in treating bipolar disorder.

12. That, while all people who commit suicide are not depressed, many people who are depressed think about or attempt taking their own life.

KEY TERMS

Depression (p. 194)

Mania (p. 196) abound w/ joyful elation
hyperactive, overconfident,
impractical, grandiose plans

Flight of ideas (p. 196) shift rapidly from topic to topic

Affective Disorders (p. 196) disabling mood disturbances

Major Depression (Unipolar) (p. 196) widespread
don't experience mania

Bipolar Depression (p. 196) both mania + depression or mania alone

Hypomania (p. 197) less severe form of mania

Cyclothymic Disorder (p. 198) frequent periods of depression + hypomania
paired sets of symptoms in periods of depression + hypomania

Dysthymic Disorder (p. 198) chronically depressed, either persistently or with periods of normal mood lasting never more than a month or 2 at a time
(insomnia, sleeping too much, feeling ineffective, pessimistic

Mourning work (p. 199)
mourner recalls memories of lost one / seperates himself from the person who has died & loosens bonds

Learned helplessness (p. 201)
the sense of helplessness + inability to control one's life acquired thru unpleasant experiences/traumas brings on dep.

Attribution (p. 203)

Neurotransmitters (p. 211)

Norepinephrine (p. 211) low levels result in depression

Serotonin (p. 211) low levels result in depression
excess causes mania

Electroconvulsive therapy (ECT) (p. 218)
dramatic depression treatment
70-130 volts

Egoistic suicide (p. 223) too few ties to society + community; feel alienated

Altruistic suicide (p. 223) sacrifice for good of society

Anomic suicide (p. 223) triggered by sudden change in a persons relations to society

STUDY QUESTIONS

GENERAL CHARACTERISTICS OF DEPRESSION AND MANIA (p. 194 - 196)

1. Give five (at least) different characteristics of depression and mania (p. 194 - 196)

FORMAL DIAGNOSTIC LISTINGS (p. 196 - 198)

2. Distinguish between the two major affective disorders (p. 196) and the other two affective disorders (p. 199 - 200) in DSM-III. What problem remains? (p. 197)

PSYCHOLOGICAL THEORIES OF DEPRESSION (p. 198 - 209)

3. According to Psychoanalytic theory, why do normal and orally fixated people react differently following a loss? Briefly list three problems with this theory. (p. 198 - 199)

4. What is the basis of depression according to Beck's cognitive theory? How well has research supported Beck in two areas? (p. 199 - 201)

5. How has Seligman applied the learned helplessness concept to depression? Explain how "attribution" was added to this theory in 1978. (p. 201 - 206)

6. The traditional learning theory of depression suggests three steps: (1) loss of reinforcers, (2) reinforcement of depressed behaviors, and (3) difficulty in acquiring new reinforcers. Explain these three steps. (p. 208 - 209)

PSYCHOLOGICAL THEORIES OF BIPOLAR DISORDER (p. 209 - 210)

7. How have most psychological theories viewed mania? Describe a study suggesting that manics try to conceal low self-esteem. (p. 209 - 210)

PHYSIOLOGICAL THEORIES OF AFFECTIVE DISORDERS (p. 210 - 215)

8. Why would evidence of genetic factors strengthen physiological theories of affective disorders? (p. 210) What has been found regarding inheritance of bipolar depression? Of unipolar depression? (p. 210 - 211)

9. What two neurotransmitters have been linked to affective disorders? What indirect clues and direct studies (two approaches) suggest this? (p. 211 - 215) (Read Box 9.4 to understand the role of neurotransmitters.)

THERAPY FOR AFFECTIVE DISORDERS (p. 215 - 219)

10. Briefly describe four psychological therapies for depression. (You will find it helpful to relate these to the corresponding theories in items 3 thru 6 above.) How effective are they? (p. 215 - 218)

11. Three somatic therapies are described. For each describe, (1) when it is used, (2) how effective it is, and (3) what side effects or problems are common. (p. 218 - 219)

SUICIDE (p. 219 - 225)

12. Do non-depressed people commit suicide? Review and be able to recognize 17 facts about suicide. (Also review some myths about suicide.) (p. 219 - 221)

13. Why is it difficult to develop good theories of suicide? Summarize two attempts. (p. 222 - 223)

14. Why has it been difficult to predict suicide from psychological texts? What have studies suggested about the (a) feelings and (b) cognitive style of suicidal individuals? (p. 223 - 224)

15. How are suicide prevention centers and psychological autopsies used in preventing suicide? (p. 223 - 225)

SELF-TEST, CHAPTER 9

MULTIPLE-CHOICE

1. Which of the following is characteristic of mania but not of depression?
   A. Lack of interest & energy
   B. Indecisiveness & difficulty concentrating
   C. Sleep problems
   D. Reckless behavior

2. One distinction between bipolar disorder and cyclothymic disorder is that
   A. Cyclothymic disorder involves depression only
   B. Cyclothymic symptoms are less pronounced
   C. Bipolar disorders never show depression and mania simultaneously
   D. Bipolar diagnoses require the presence of delusions

3. According to psychoanalytic theory depression develops if a person
   A. Is too dependent to emotionally let go of a lost loved one
   B. Becomes angry at having lost a lived one
   C. Has unresolved, unconscious, conflicts regarding a lost loved one
   D. Identifies with a lost loved one

4. Which of the following theories argues that depression results when people harshly blame themselves for everything that goes wrong.
   A. Psychoanalytic theory
   B. Beck's theory
   C. Physiological theory
   D. Learning theory

5. Seligman's early research showed that rats became "helpless"

A. Whenever they were given very strong shocks
B. Whenever they were shocked repeatedly
C. When they could not escape shock
D. When they had no earlier experience with shock

6. Seligman's attributional theory argues that depression is a result of

A. Physical attributes of the individual
B. Always having to attribute failure to something or somebody
C. Not being aware of one's attributions
D. The manner in which people attribute failure

7. The critical point of recent research on the self-esteem of manic individuals was that

A. They did not overtly admit to low self-esteem
B. They had low self-esteem only when in manic episodes
C. Their self-esteem was higher than that of normals
D. Their self-esteem matched that of depressed individuals

8. Research on genetic transmission of affective disorders shows

A. High heritability for both bipolar and unipolar depression
B. Low heritability for both bipolar and unipolar depression
C. Higher heritability for bipolar depression
D. Higher heritability for unipolar depression

9. Which of the following has NOT been shown effective in treating depression

A. Psychoanalysis
B. Beck's cognitive approach
C. Electroconvulsive shock
D. Tricyclic drugs

10. Which of the following statements about suicide is true.
    A. Blacks are more likely to attempt suicide than whites
    B. Women are more likely to kill themselves than men
    C. Suicide is among the leading causes of death among college students
    D. Mental health professionals are less likely to attempt suicide

11. The ____________ method studies suicide by looking at notes left by people who committed suicide
    A. Psychological autopsy
    B. Egoistic
    C. Demographic
    D. Graphometric analysis

SHORT ANSWER

1. List five characteristics of depression in addition to feeling sad. sleep thoughts of suicide
lack of energy weight gain / loss inability to concentrate

2. Identify two differences found in affectively disordered individuals which are NOT reflected in the DSM-III labels.

3. What is meant by asking "Are attributions relevant?" in evaluating learned helplessness research?

4. Learning theories have failed to show whether depression is a result or a cause of . . .

5. Most psychological theorists suggest that manic episodes be viewed or interpreted as . . .

6. Neurotransmitter theories of affective disorders developed out of research which showed that . . .

7. Describe two strategies used in research on the relationship between neurotransmitters and depression.

8. What do therapists do to treat depression based on cognitive theories of it's cause?

9. The following is an example of Durkheim's ___________ suicide

> Joe was a straight-A student who was highly-motivated to become a lawyer. He killed himself after he flunked out of law school his first semester.

10. What two personality characteristics are most highly correlated with suicide on psychological tests?

ANSWERS TO SELF-TEST, CHAPTER 9

MULTIPLE-CHOICE

1. D (p. 196)
2. B (p. 198)
3. A (p. 199)
4. B (p. 200)
5. C (p. 201)
6. D (p. 203)
7. A (p. 209-210)
8. C (p. 210)
9. A (p. 215)
10. C (p. 220)
11. A (p. 224)

SHORT ANSWER

1. Changes in sleep, eating, activity level. Loss of interest, energy, concentration. Negative feelings about self with thoughts of suicide. (p. 194)

2. Severe vs. hypomanic episodes. Presence or absence of psychotic delusions & hallucinations. Presence or absence of melancholic symptoms. (p. 197)

3. Asks if people actually spend much time and energy considering the causes of their behavior? (p. 206-207)

4. Low rate of positive reinforcement (p. 209)

5. Defenses or attempts to avoid depression. (p. 209)

6. Drugs which relieved depression also increased levels of specific neurotransmitters. (p. 212-213)

7. 1) Study metabolic by-products of neurotransmitters in the blood, urine, etc. 2)Study whether drugs that effect neurotransmitters also effect the disorders. (p. 213-214)

8. Help clients identify and change their beliefs using logical analysis, providing contrary examples or experiences, etc. (p. 21-217)

9. Anomic (p. 223)

10. Hopelessness and rigid or constricted thought (p. 224)

10 Personality Disorders and Sociopathy

OVERVIEW

The previous chapter completed the text's discussion of emotional problems. The four chapters in that section studied anxiety, stress, and depression, and the problems that arise from those emotions.

Chapter 10 begins four chapters on a cluster of "Social problems". These problems are characterized by particular behaviors or personality traits which are of considerable concern to society and/or to the individual. Generally social problems are not considered "mental illnesses" as the term is commonly used.

Chapter 10 covers personality disorders characterized by persistent personality traits that cause concern. Examples include persistent social withdrawal, self-centeredness, and criminal activity. The remaining chapters cover specific behaviors of social concern. Chapter 11 deals with substance use disorders such as drug and alcohol abuse. Chapters 12 and 13 deal with sexual problems which are divided into sexual disorders or deviations (such as fetishism and rape) and sexual dysfunctions or inadequacies (such as impotence).

After chapter 13 the text will discuss an entirely different kind of problem, schizophrenia, in which individuals are said to be "out of contact with reality".

CHAPTER SUMMARY

Personality disorders are defined as inflexible and maladaptive personality traits which impair the individual's functioning. Only one personality disorder is well understood or studied and most of the chapter focuses on this disorder; antisocial personality disorder or sociopathy.

The chapter begins by discussing DSM-III's definition of personality disorders and then defines the Specific Personality Disorders.

Antisocial Personality Disorder (Sociopathy), the only widely studied personality disorder, involves a lack of shame or sense of responsibility. Sociopaths repeatedly engage in criminal or unethical activities and do not form genuine emotional relationships.

Theory and Research on the Etiology of Sociopathy includes several areas. Research on the families of sociopaths shows they provided inconsistent or little discipline and that fathers themselves were antisocial. Research also suggests a genetic predisposition to sociopathy.

Several research areas focus on sociopaths' inability to inhibit activities that lead to punishment. Some sociopaths show EEG brain waves suggesting failure of inhibitory processes. Sociopaths are slow to learn to avoid electric shock but do avoid if artificially aroused. Physiologically they seem to show little arousal but closer study suggests they anticipate and physiologically tune out stress. They have difficulty planning or changing their patterns of responding similar to the deficits of frontal lobe brain damaged individuals.

Therapies for Personality Disorders typically are not successful. These people have long standing problems and rarely seek help. Except for sociopathy, treatment is infrequently studied or attempted. Psychological and somatic treatment of sociopaths has been unsuccessful. Prisons remain the common way of handling sociopaths but are used primarily to punish and isolate them.

STUDY OBJECTIVES

After studying Chapter 10 you should know

1. That personality disorders are characterized by inflexible and maladaptive traits that interfere with functioning. This Axis II diagnosis is controversial and less reliable than many other diagnostic categories.

2. That Antisocial personality disorder or sociopathy is characterized by antisocial behavior which occurs with no sense of responsibility or shame.

3. That evidence suggests that the family plays a role in the development of antisocial behavior in that inconsistent discipline, lack of affection, and parental rejection are predictive of the disorder.

4. That evidence also suggests that genetic factors play a role in etiology of antisocial behavior.

5. That clinical experience and laboratory studies show that sociopaths do not seem to learn from experience or to respond to punishment. Although there is evidence to indicate that they will respond to certain types of punishments.

6. That a number of theorists suggests that sociopaths are underaroused and engage in antisocial behavior in order to obtain adequate stimulation.

7. That the attempts at treating antisocial personality disorder have been notably ineffective.

KEY TERMS

Personality disorder (p. 230) long-standing, inflexible which impair social & occupational functioning but not contact w/ reality

Paranoid personality disorder (p. 230)
appear cold & humorless, extremely jealous, suspicious

Schizoid personality disorder (p. 231) difficulty forming social relationships; dull & lonely (in contact w/ reality)

Schizotypal personality disorder (p. 231) has interpersonal difficulties of ↑ also superstitious, may have depersonalization, illusions (sees forces/people aren't there) can be psychotic. may be mild schizo.

Borderline personality disorder (p. 231)
instability in relationships, mood, self-image. Can't bear to be alone. Little concern for others. Subject to depression & emptiness

Histrionic personality disorder (p. 232) overly dramatic interpersonal problems - constant demands on others. More frequently in ♀

Narcissistic personality disorder (p. 232) Grandiose. Crave attention from others. Self-centered
(Coping w/ shortcomings lacking parental support psychoa.)

Avoidant personality disorder (p. 232) very sensitive to social rejection & humiliation. Yearn for affection but resist relationships. Low self-esteem devalue achievements

Dependent personality disorder (p. 232) lack self-confidence Very passive. Unable to make demands. "inferiority complex" more common in ♀

Compulsive personality disorder (p. 232) perfectionists work-oriented. Difficulty making decisions. Relationships poor very serious & formal. ♂

Passive-aggressive personality disorder (p. 233) indirectly resist demands of others. Procrastinate & "forget"
A hostile way of controlling others without ass. respons. for their own anger

Antisocial personality disorder (p. 233) charming & habitual liar no regard for others, shows no remorse
unable to form relationships & take respons. doesn't respond to punishment

Sociopath, psychopath (p. 233)

Cleckley (p. 235)

Retrospective reports (p. 237)

Electroencephalogram (EEG) (P. 238)

STUDY QUESTIONS

1. How does DSM-III define personality disorders as a group? Briefly identify two practical and one theoretical problem with this definition. (p. 230)

SPECIFIC PERSONALITY DISORDERS (p. 230 - 233)

2. Identify and briefly define eleven personality disorders (including Antisocial Personality Disorder). You will find it helpful to note the three clusters into which they fall. (p. 230 - 233)

ANTISOCIAL PERSONALITY DISORDER (SOCIOPATHY) (p. 233 - 236)

3. Compare the definitions of sociopathy offered by Cleckley and DSM-III. Why has it been difficult to conduct research on sociopaths? (p. 233 - 236)

THEORY AND RESEARCH ON THE ETIOLOGY OF SOCIOPATHY (p. 236 - 244)

4. What have studies found about the role of the family in sociopathy? (Look for affection, discipline, and father's behavior) (p. 236 - 238)

5. What has been found in twin and adoptee studies. What has been found in studies of central nervous system activity? (p. 238 - 240)

6. Describe the general procedure used by Lykken (and others) to study avoidance learning and sociopathy. What was found by early studies and by later studies? (p. 240 - 242)

7. Researchers have studied arousal and planning in sociopaths. Describe the results and implications of each area. (p. 243 - 244)

THERAPIES FOR PERSONALITY DISORDERS (p. 245 - 247)

8. How effective is therapy for most personality disorders and why? How do behavior therapists try to treat personality disorders? (p. 245)

9. How effective is psychotherapy with sociopaths and why? How effective are somatic treatments? (p. 245 - 246)

10. How effective are prisons in treating (rehabilitating) sociopaths? What seems to be the current social view of the role of prisons? (p. 246 - 247)

SELF-TEST, CHAPTER 10

MULTIPLE-CHOICE

1. Which of the labels below best fits the following; Joe's may act sad one minute and angry the next. He seems to have no idea what he wants out of life. He says he cannot stand being alone yet he gets into violent fights with his friends over minor matters. He attempted suicide when his marriage broke up due to his violent mood shifts and impulsive gambling.
   A. Schizotypal personality
   B. Borderline personality
   C. Histrionic personality
   D. Narcissistic personality

2. Which of the following terms means essentially the same thing as the term "Antisocial Personality Disorder"?
   A. Sociopath
   B. Criminal
   C. Schizotypal Personality
   D. XYY Syndrome

3. Only one of the two of antisocial personality disorders described in the text
   A. Really cared about other people
   B. Had been convicted of criminal acts
   C. Was homosexual
   D. Had been normal until well into adulthood

4. A major problem in research on antisocial personalities is that
   A. Much of it was based on outdated definitions of antisocial personality
   B. Civil rights laws limit the methods that can be used
   C. It is difficult to know if participants are being truthful
   D. Many studies were done on criminals

5. Researchers have often used ____________ to study the role of the family in producing antisocial personalities.
   A. Identical twins
   B. Participant observation
   C. Longitudinal measures
   D. Retrospective reports

6. "Incidental" learning as used in Lykken's avoidance learning research is called incidental because
   A. Avoidance had no effect of the outcome of the research
   B. Successful avoidance was not possible
   C. Subjects were not told avoidance was possible
   D. Subjects received no benefit from learning to avoid

7. Research indicates that sociopaths are more likely than normals to learn to avoid
   A. Strong aversive events
   B. Loss of money
   C. When consequences are uncertain
   D. Social punishment

8. Studies of autonomic nervous system arousal in sociopaths indicate that they
   A. Have no emotional response to aversive stimuli
   B. Anticipate and tune out aversive stimuli
   C. Are emotionally overwhelmed by aversive stimuli
   D. Are emotionally attracted to aversive stimuli

9. Behavior therapists have generally treated most forms of personality disorder by
   A. Redefining the problem in more behavioral terms
   B. Using money as a reinforcer to shape socially desirable behavior
   C. Working with teachers to keep children from developing the problems in the first place
   D. Incarcerating people until middle age

10. Treatment of antisocial personality disorders
    A. Has rarely been attempted
    (B.) Has been generally unsuccessful
    C. Has improved recently due to new drugs
    D. Has improved recently due to new behavioral therapy methods

11. At present prison based programs to rehabilitate sociopaths
    (A.) Are of little interest
    B. Are based on behavioral principles
    C. Have been shown to be generally ineffective
    D. Are successful in the majority of cases

SHORT ANSWER

1. Personality disorders are defined in terms of pers. traits as opposed to other DSM-III labels which are defined in terms of (hopefully) specific behaviors.

2. Define "Histrionic personality disorder". overly dramatic - ~~must be center of attraction~~ more common in ♀. Constant in demands

3. List four classic characteristics of sociopaths in addition to antisocial behavior. superficial charm - ave or above intelligence
unreliable - no sense of respons. lack of remorse / no shame
untruthful + insincere

4. Research on the role of the family finds that sociopaths tend to come from families characterized by . . .
rejection, no affection, inconsistent discipline

5. Why are genetic correlates of sociopathic behavior NOT shown by twin studies which found higher concordances of sociopathy in identical than fraternal twins of sociopaths?

6. The slow-wave activity found in the EEGs of many sociopaths suggests . . .

7. Describe the procedure used to study avoidance learning in sociopaths.

8. How is the "underarousal" view of sociopathy strengthened by results of avoidance learning studies where sociopaths were injected with adrenalin?

9. Why is there little research on therapies for personality disorders?

10. It can be argued that incarceration is an effective treatment for sociopaths because . . . .

ANSWERS TO SELF-TEST, CHAPTER 10

MULTIPLE-CHOICE

1. B (p. 231)
2. A (p. 233)
3. B (p. 234-235)
4. D (p. 234)
5. D (p. 237)
6. C (p. 240)
7. B (p. 241-242)
8. B (p. 243)
9. A (p. 245)
10. B (p. 245)
11. A (p. 246-247)

SHORT ANSWER

1. Personality traits (which are inflexible & maladaptive) (p. 230)

2. Label for individuals with overly dramatic, excessive emotions that are immature, manipulative, irresponsible. (p. 232)

3. Charming, intelligent, no shame, irresponsible, poor judgment, no lasting friends, no symptoms such as anxiety or delusions, etc. (List, p. 235-236)

4. Rejection, lack of affection, inconsistent discipline, antisocial fathers. (p. 237)

5. Higher concordances among same-sex fraternal twins point to similar child rearing practices (p. 238)

6. Lack of inhibitory mechanisms similar to children (p. 239-240)

7. Person is asked to learn the correct series of choices and told that punishment will, sometimes, follow errors. Actually punishment follows only one of the possible errors. (p. 240)

8. Adrenalin, which increases arousal, improved the avoidance of sociopaths but reduced avoidance of normals (presumably by overarousing them) (p. 240-242)

9. There are few opportunities to work with them as they do not typically seek therapy. They do not seek or form therapeutic relationships well. (p. 245)

10. They often become less disruptive after about age forty. (p. 247)

11 Substance Use Disorders

OVERVIEW

Chapter 11 is the second of four chapters on social problems. These problems involve particular behavioral or personality patterns of social concern.

The previous chapter (Chapter 10) covered personality disorders in which persistent personality traits cause concern to either the individual or society. The most obvious personality disorder is the antisocial personality characterized by antisocial behavior and especially by lack of guilt over that behavior.

Chapter 11 will discuss substance abuse disorders including abuse of alcohol, marijuana, nicotine, and hard drugs. Substance abuse problems are particular behaviors rather than general traits like personality disorders but both share the characteristic of being of at least as much concern to society as to the individual with the disorder.

The next two chapters will deal with sexual problems. Chapter 12 discusses sexual disorders or deviant sexual behaviors. Chapter 13 discusses sexual dysfunctions or difficulties in maintaining normal sexual behaviors.

CHAPTER SUMMARY

Drugs have always been used, and abused, to alter mood and consciousness. Contemporary practice distinguishes between substance abuse which effects daily functioning and substance dependence or addiction which produces physiological changes leading to physical tolerance (or decreasing effects) and withdrawl reactions. The chapter discusses the social, psychological, and physical effects of five groups of commonly abused substances.

Alcoholism is a widespread social problem. Alcohol produces short-term effects including poor judgement and coordination and long-term effects including addiction and physical deterioration. A variety of psychological and physiological theories have been offered for why alcoholics both start and maintain their drinking. Similarly a variety of therapy approaches have been developed.

The so-called hard drugs are illegal, often addictive, drugs and include both Sedatives such as narcotics and barbiturates, and Stimulants such as amphetamines and cocaine. As with alcoholism, there are a variety of physiological and psychological approaches to understanding and treating abuse of these drugs.

Nicotine and Cigarette Smoking is still common despite increasing evidence of health risks. Recent evidence suggests nicotine is addictive at least when used heavily. There have been many attempts to both prevent and treat nicotine abuse.

Marijuana is commonly used to produce a "high". Stronger forms of marijuana plus increased social usage is producing evidence of physical and, possibly, psychological dangers of long term use. Debate continues over whether it is addictive and over its possible uses in medical treatment.

PCP is a new drug which produces unpredictable, violent, and dangerous behavior. LSD and Other Psychedelics were originally studied, and are now abused, for their mind altering properties.

STUDY OBJECTIVES

After studying Chapter 11 you should know

1. That substance abuse involves abuse of a drug to the extent that in interferes with social, familial,, or occupational functioning, and that substance dependence involves a physiological addiction to a drug.

2. That addiction is a physiological process which is evidenced by withdrawal reactions and evidence of increased tolerance.

3. That alcohol is an addicting drug that exacts a high cost from many individuals and from our society.

4. That alcohol has short-term physiological effects with its influence mediated by cognitive expectancies. The long-term consequences can be quite severe both psychologically and physiologically.

5. That sedatives ("downers") reduce the body's responsiveness. They include organic narcotics and synthetic barbiturates.

6. That the narcotics (opium and its derivatives morphine and heroin) are highly addicting and have important social consequences. For example criminal behavior may result from an addict's attempt to maintain the expensive habit.

7. That stimulants (amphetamine and cocaine) are "uppers" that heighten alertness and increase autonomic activity. Increasingly they are considered addictive.

8. That available treatments for addicts are not particularly successful.

9. Cigarette smoking is a tremendous health problem. Prevention may be the best treatment because it is a very difficult habit to stop.

10. That marijuana interferes with cognitive functioning and psychomotor performance and appears to have some adverse physical effects with long-term use.

11. That LSD and other psychedelics produce a state that was once thought to mimic psychosis, and is characterized sometimes by dramatic changes in perception and cognition.

KEY TERMS

Substance abuse & dependence (p. 250)

Addiction (p. 250)

Alcoholism (p. 251)

Fetal alcohol syndrome (p. 256)

Delirium tremens (DTs) (p. 257)

Delay of reward gradient (p. 258)

Detoxification (p. 261)

Covert sensitization (p. 262)

Aversion therapy (p. 262)

Narcotics (p. 264)

Opium (p. 264)

Morphine (p. 264)

Heroin (p. 264)

Endorphins (p. 265

Barbiturates (p. 265)

Amphetamines (p. 267)

Cocaine (p. 267)

Heroin substitutes (Methadone) (p. 271)

Heroin antagonists (p. 271)

Nicotine (p. 274)

Rapid-smoking treatment (p. 275)

Marijuana (& Hashish) (p. 277)

Psychedelics (p. 282)

LSD (p. 282)

Flashbacks (p. 283)

PCP (p. 284)

STUDY QUESTIONS

1. Identify and distinguish between two categories of substance use. (p. 250)

ALCOHOLISM (p. 251 - 264)

2. How much of a problem is alcoholism from a social and legal point of view? What behaviors distinguish alcohol abuse and alcohol dependency? (p. 251 - 253)

3. What are the short-term and long-term effects of alcohol (p. 253 - 257)

4. Briefly summarize four theories of alcoholism discussed in the text. (For the learning view, what kind of distress is reduced by alcohol?) (p. 257 - 261)

5. Briefly describe five treatments for alcoholism. (Note that most programs combine several of these treatments.) What has been the general problem with attempts to treat alcoholism? (p. 261 - 264)

SEDATIVES AND STIMULANTS (p. 264 - 272)

6. The text identifies two groups of sedatives and two groups of stimulants. For each group, describe (1) short-term effects, (2) long-term effects, and (3) withdrawal effects. (p. 264 - 270)

7. List a number of physiological and psychological factors that have been suggested in drug abuse. (p. 270)

8. Describe Therapy for drug use including the two stages involved and two components of the second stage. (p. 270 - 272)

NICOTINE AND CIGARETTE SMOKING (p. 272 - 277)

9. How common and how serious is cigarette smoking? What evidence suggests that nicotine is addicting, at least for some smokers. (p. 272 - 275)

10. How effective are current smoking treatment programs? Describe one promising treatment. Give three suggestions for improving efforts to deal with cigarette smoking. (p. 275 - 277)

MARIJUANA (p. 277 - 282)

11. How commonly do people use marijuana? Identify two psychological and two somatic effects of marijuana. (p. 277 - 280)

12. Is marijuana addictive? Why is the interaction of marijuana and other drugs (especially alcohol) of concern. (p. 280 - 281)

LSD AND OTHER PSYCHEDELICS (p. 282 - 285)

13. How were LSD and other psychedelics studied and viewed prior too 1960? What happened to change this? (p. 282 - 283)

14. According to research, are psychedelics addictive? Explain how situational and personality factors influence their effects. (p. 283)

15. What are flashbacks? Describe a possible psychological explanation for flashbacks. (p. 283 - 285)

SELF-TEST, CHAPTER 11

MULTIPLE-CHOICE

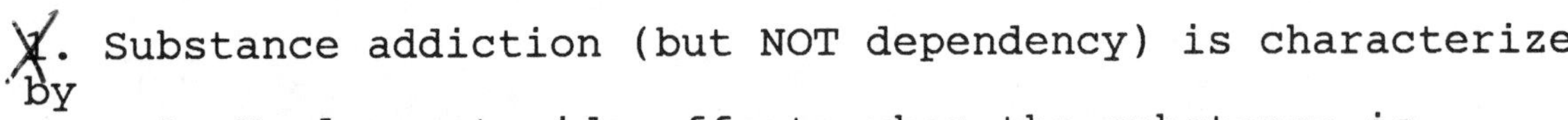

1. Substance addiction (but NOT dependency) is characterized by
   A. Unpleasant side-effects when the substance is withdrawn
   B. Strong desire to continue taking the substance
   C. Progressively larger doses needed for effect
   D. All of the above

2. Recent research indicates that drinking small amounts of alcohol produces
   A. Increased aggression
   B. Increased sexual arousal
   C. Decreased anxiety
   D. Varying effects depending on beliefs about it's effects

3. Delirium tremens
   A. Occurs only when alcohol is withdrawn after prolonged drinking
   B. Produces symptoms which are frightening but not dangerous
   C. Involves a prolonged sleep resembling coma in which body temperature drops
   D. Occurs only in physiologically predisposed individuals

4. Research into possible physiological predispositions to alcoholism suggests that
   A. Alcoholism only appears to run in families because children learn alcoholic behaviors from growing up with alcoholic parents
   B. Alcoholics may inherit a predisposition to tolerate alcohol
   C. Women are especially likely to inherit a predisposition to alcoholism
   D. There is no obvious genetic or physiological predisposition to alcoholism

5. A general problem with attempts to treat alcoholism has been the failure to
   - A. Deal with the side-effects of alcohol withdrawl
   - B. Consider methods of teaching alcoholics to become controlled social drinkers
   - C. Recognize that people may become alcoholic for many different reasons
   - D. Recognize the social costs of alcoholism

6. The effects of moderate doses of amphetamines include
   - A. Increased energy, euphoria, and reduced appetite
   - B. Drowsiness, calmness, reduced sensitivity to pain
   - C. Dreaminess, unusual & often enjoyable sensory experiences
   - D. Agitation, bizarre experiences, aggression

7. Chemical drug therapy programs for drug abusers have
   - A. Proven highly effective
   - B. Been used primarily with heroin addicts
   - C. Been effective only in treating non-addictive drugs
   - D. Not been widely attempted or investigated

8. Research into the addictive properties of nicotine suggests that
   - A. It is not clearly addictive
   - B. It is just as clearly addictive as other drugs such as heroin
   - C. It is addictive for heavy smokers
   - D. There is no general agreement and further research is needed

9. A promising new method for treating cigarette smoking involves
   - A. Having the individual smoke rapidly in a closed room
   - B. Forced withdrawl in a hospital while using drugs to minimize withdrawl symptoms
   - C. Social skills training to reduce stresses that cause the individual to desire cigarettes
   - D. Substituting chewing tobacco for cigarettes

10. Which of the following drugs appears NOT to be physiologically addicting
   A. Amphetamines
   B. Morphine
   C. Nicotine
   (D) LSD

SHORT ANSWER

1. List four indicators of dependence on alcohol.
increased tolerance withdrawl symptoms
daily drinking can't stop

2. What does the text conclude about descriptions of alcoholic stages such as Jellinek's?

3. The delay of reinforcement gradient is used to explain what in learning theories of alcoholism?

4. Disulfiram or Antabuse can discourage alcoholics from drinking by doing what? makes a person vomit

5. According to the best current evidence, can alcoholics learn to drink in moderation?

6. Describe the physiological mechanism apparently responsible for the effects (and withdrawl effects of opium based drugs.

7. List two substances which can have fatal withdrawl side effects. alcohol
barbiturates

8. Describe the immediate effects of cocaine.

9. Psychological theories of drug abuse typically seek to explain what?

10. What are the common reasons for use of marijuana?

11. What factors appear responsible for LSD "flashbacks"?

ANSWERS TO SELF-TEST, CHAPTER 11

MULTIPLE-CHOICE

1. C (p. 250)
2. D (p. 254)
3. A (p. 257)
4. B (p. 260)
5. C (p. 263
6. A (p. 267)
7. B (p. 271)
8. C (p. 274)
9. A (p. 275)
10. D (p. 283)

SHORT ANSWER

1. Regular daily drinking, Inability to stop, binges, tolerance, withdrawl symptoms, drinking to relieve withdrawl, etc. (p. 252-253)

2. Progression is less consistent than the descriptions imply. (p. 256)

3. Why long-term negative effects of alcohol are less effective than short-term positive effects. (p. 258)

4. Produces violent vomiting if individual drinks alcohol after taking it (p. 261)

5. Evidence is controversial but apparently some (only) can do so. (p. 263)

6. Drug simulates body's own pain-relieving endorphins but also causes the body to decrease production leading to withdrawl effects. (p. 265)

7. Alcohol (p. 257) and barbiturates (p. 266)

8. Reduces pain, heightened sensory awareness, euphoria, sexual desire, self-confidence and energy. (p. 268-269)

9. Why particular kinds of people are especially susceptible to drug abuse. (p. 270)

10. Feelings of being high and relaxed as well as social and political implications. (p. 278-279)

11. Combination of situations, expectations, and personality patterns encourages sensitivity to non-real experiences which become self-fulfilling. (p. 285)

12 Psychosexual Disorders: Gender Identity Disorders and the Paraphilias

OVERVIEW

Chapter 12 is the third of four chapters on social problems. Generally these problems are not considered "mental illnesses" as such but involve particular behaviors or personality traits which are of concern to society and/or to the individual. Chapter 10 discussed personality disorders, especially antisocial personality disorders. Antisocial behavior is defined as a "problem" by society not the individual criminal. Chapter 11 discussed substance abuse problems which concern both society and the individual to varying degrees. Social and individual concerns about these problems can change dramatically as has happened with cigarette smoking.

This chapter and the following one will deal with sexual problems. Sexual problems are commonly divided into two groups. This chapter will discuss sexual deviations. As the term implies, sexual deviations refer to sexual activities that society considers deviant or aberrant. Like the personality disorders and substance abuse disorders of the last two chapters, defining a sexual activity as "deviant" involves a social or individual value judgment. Again our social and individual concerns may change. Currently our views on homosexuality are changing and these changes are reflected in changing DSM labels.

Chapter 13 will look at sexual dysfunctions. Sexual dysfunctions are much more common sexual problems involving difficulty in engaging in or enjoying normal sexual functioning. Sexual dysfunctions include premature orgasm, vaginismus, and inhibited sexual desire or arousal. Generally sexual dysfunctions are of most concern to the individual experiencing them.

CHAPTER SUMMARY

DSM-III identifies three groups of psychosexual disorders. In Gender Identity Disorders individuals have a sense of themselves as being of one sex although they are anatomically the other sex. Such individuals wish they had the body of the other sex and could live as such. Such individuals may seek sex-change surgery to make their physical anatomy consistent with their inner sense of themselves. Behavior therapy can also help them change their behaviors, sexual fantasies, etc. to match their anatomy. Such individuals were often encouraged to dress and act as the opposite sex which suggests the importance of early learning in how we view ourselves sexually.

In The Paraphilias the individual persistently requires unusual activities of fantasies in order to experience sexual arousal or gratification. The individual may repeatedly seek gratification through handling intimate articles, dressing in particular ways or through sexual activities involving pain, children, etc. Behavior therapists treat such problems using aversion therapy to reduce the unwanted attraction plus social skills training to enable normal sexual relations.

Rape is not considered a paraphilia in DSM-III. Many professionals view it as an act of violence rather than a sexual act. Still it is of considerable social concern and causes much psychological trauma to victims.

Social and professional views on homosexuality are changing. DSM-III does not include a category of homosexuality but does include Ego-dystonic Homosexuality for individuals who are unhappy as homosexuals and wish to be heterosexuals. Even this label is the source of much controversy.

STUDY OBJECTIVES

After studying Chapter 12 you should know

1. that gender identity disorders refer to instances where one believes that one is the opposite of one's anatomical sex.

2. That transsexualism and gender identity disorder of childhood are the two gender identity disorders listed in DSM-III.

3. That the two major treatments for gender identity disorders -- sex-change surgery and alterations in gender identity -- are quite controversial.

4. That paraphilias involve a deviation in the object of sexual arousal.

5. That the more common paraphilias include fetishism, transvestism, incest, pedophilia, voyeurism, exhibitionism, rape, and sadism and masochism.

6. That rape is typically more a crime of aggression and dominance than of sex, and that it can have a tremendously adverse impact on the victim.

7. That little is known about the specific etiology or the most effective treatments of the paraphilias.

8. That there has been a history of debate as to whether homosexuality should be considered abnormal. DSM-III indicates that discomfort with a homosexual orientation is due to social prejudices.

KEY TERMS

Psychosexual disorders (p. 288) sexual thoughts, feeling + actions regarded as abnormal + dysfunctional

Axis I

Gender identity disorder (p. 289)
transsexualism
gender identity disorder

Transsexualism (p. 289) adult w/ persistent, deep sense of discomfort in this anatomic sex, felt this way for more than 2 yrs.

Gender identity disorder of childhood (p. 290) profoundly feminine boys / masc. girls. Behaviors don't fit culture's rules. -Mothers have taken sex hormones during pregnancy

Sex-change surgery (p. 291)

Paraphilia (p. 295) preference for use of nonhuman object for arousal
involve real or simulated suffering or humiliation
repetitive sexual activity w/ nonconsenting partners (activity may be imaginable)

♂ Fetishism (p. 295)
sexually enthralled by an inanimate object or a nongenital part of a person

Transvestite (p. 296) ♂ is sexually aroused by dressing in ♀'s clothing while still regarding himself a ♂

Incest (p. 297)

♂ Pedophilia (p. 298) derive gratification through physical / sexual contact with prepubertal children

Voyeurism (p. 298) looking at unsuspecting people

♂ Exhibitionism (p. 299) exposes genitals to an unsuspecting purpose (no attempt at further sex. activity

Forcible (& statutory) rape (p. 301)

(rape between a ♂ and a ♀ who is a minor

Sexual sadism and masochism (p. 303) sadist - pleasure by inflicting pain on his/her partner - masochists gratified by being subject to pain masochists outnumber sadists

Orgasmic reorientation (p. 306) help paraphiliacs respond sexually to stimuli or sit. that for them do not have the accustomed appeal - confronted w/ conventional stimulus while they respond sexually for other undesireable reasons

Ego dystonic homosexuality (p. 309)

homosexual who finds his arousal to be a persistent form of distress - wishes to become heterosexual

STUDY QUESTIONS

GENDER IDENTITY DISORDERS (p. 289 - 295)

1. Define transsexualism, noting two things which it is NOT (p. 289)

2. Summarize three lines of evidence regarding this gender identity disorder of childhood. Give two reasons why we should not be too concerned about children who play "inappropriately". (p. 290 - 291)

3. Describe two therapies for gender identity disorders pointing out problems in evaluating their effectiveness. (p. 291 - 295)

THE PARAPHILIAS (p. 295 - 309)

4. What are paraphilias? Distinguish between paraphilias and the unusual sexual urges that most people feel from time to time. (p. 295)

5. Omitting rape, describe seven forms of paraphilia and note any background or personality factors usually associated with it. Describe the psychoanalytic and learning views of paraphilias (these are described in essentially similar terms for many of the paraphilias>). (p. 295 - 305)

6. Define forcible (as opposed to statutory) rape. What are the effects of rape on victims? (p. 301 - 302)

7. What is the motivation of the rapist? What are Brownmiller's views on this topic? What relationship has been suggested between rape and cultural stereotypes of masculinity and femininity? (p. 302 - 303)

8. Describe two goals of therapy for paraphilias and the kind of methods used for each. (p. 305 - 306)

9. Describe two approached to treating rapists and the effectiveness of each. Describe the immediate and long-term goals in counseling rape victims. (p. 306 - 308)

EGO-DYSTONIC HOMOSEXUALITY (p. 309 - 311)

10. What position did DSM-II take regarding homosexuality? Why did this change? What is the position of DSM-III? (p. 309)

11. Is the new DSM-III category really be as accepting of homosexuality as it appears? What other view may be taken? What similar comment can be made about past theory and research? (p. 309 - 311)

SELF-TEST, CHAPTER 12

MULTIPLE-CHOICE

1. Children who are encouraged to dress and play like members of the opposite sex typically grow up to become
   A. Transexuals
   B. Homosexuals
   C. Paraphiliacs
   D. Sexually normal

2. Individuals with ____________ commonly experience their sexual attraction as involuntary and irresistible
   A. Fetishism
   B. Pedophilia
   C. Exhibitionism
   D. All of the above

3. In general, individuals with paraphilias are
   A. Characterized by stronger than normal sexual drives
   B. Unable to become sexually aroused under any conditions
   C. Only aroused by bizarre imagry or actions
   D. None of the above are common in paraphilias

4. Transvestites, but not transsexuals
   A. Feel they are the opposite sex than they are anatomically
   B. Dress in clothes of the opposite sex
   C. Are typically also homosexual
   D. Are sexually aroused by dressing as the opposite sex

5. In voyeurism, sexual arousal usually
   A. Involves the risk or anticipation of being detected
   B. Is accompanied by fantasies of being seduced
   C. Requires inflicting physical pain on others
   D. Does not occur

6. In cases of rape it is typical that
   A. The rapist was momentarily overcome by sexual desires
   B. The victim is young and attractive
   C. The victim experiences few after-effects
   D. The rapist was motivated by both sexual and aggressive urges

7. Sexual activities of sadistic individuals typically
   A. Result in severe injury or death of their partners
   B. Involve willing masochistic partners
   C. Involve both giving and receiving pain
   D. All of the above

8. Therapy for sex offenders
   A. Has not been studied seriously
   B. Has advanced greatly in recent years
   C. Has often been punitive
   D. Is not needed as they rarely repeat their crimes

9. Ego-dystonic homosexuals are, by definition,
   A. Out of touch with their true inner sexual urges
   B. Emotionally and sexually immature
   C. Unhappy with their homosexuality
   D. Not sexually active

10. The text criticizes DSM-III's label "Ego-dystonic Homosexuality" because
   A. Psychophysiological measures are used in defining it
   B. It is not logically consistent
   C. It can be applied to all homosexuals
   D. It fails to consider the causes of homosexuality

SHORT ANSWER

1. Define gender identity disorder.

2. Describe in general the psychological procedures used to treat gender identity disorders.

3. What is the cause of many paraphilias according to learning theorys?

4. How dangerous to others are exhibitionists and voyeurs?

5. What are the psychological effects of rape on the victim?

6. What can we learn about human sexuality from studying rape and other unconventional sexual behaviors according to the text?

7. Describe procedures commonly used in treating paraphilias.

8. Psychological treatment for paraphilias is complicated by the fact that . . .

9. Identify at least three goals of therapy for rape victims.

10. What is the cause of ego-dystonic homosexuality?

ANSWERS TO SELF-TEST, CHAPTER 12

MULTIPLE-CHOICE

1. D (p. 290-291) 2. D (p. 295-300) 3. C (p. 295)
4. D (p. 296-297) 5. A (p. 298-299) 6. D (p. 302-303)
7. B (p. 303) 8. C (p. 308) 9. C (p. 309)
10. B (p. 309)

SHORT ANSWER

1. Label describing people who inwardly feel or believe themselves the opposite sex than they are anatomically. (p. 289)

2. Behavioral methods used to shape specific behaviors and sexual arousal patterns. (p. 293)

3. The object or activity has come to be paired with sexual arousal through classical conditioning. (p. 297 & 301)

4. Not very. These individuals rarely attempt to touch or contact others sexually. (p. 299-300)

5. Terrified & violated during attack. Afterwards tense, humiliated, angry or guilty. Nightmares, continued fears, sexual difficulties common. (p. 301-302)

6. Sexuality can serve many purposes. Some "sexual" behaviors are better understood in nonsexual terms. (p. 303)

7. Behavioral procedures tailored to individual but often using aversive procedures to decrease inappropriate attractions and procedures to condition appropriate attractions and/or teach social skills. (p. 305-306)

8. Individuals engage in these behaviors for many different reasons. (p. 306)

9. Help with immediate emotional crisis, legal and medical procedures. Afterwards help deal with feelings about attack, relations with other males and their reactions. (p. 307-308)

10. Social biases against homosexuality that are accepted by the individual. (p. 309)

13 Psychosexual Dysfunctions

OVERVIEW

This is the last of four chapters devoted to social problems. So far, the chapters have covered a wide range of behaviors and lifestyles which are not normally considered "mental illnesses" but which are objectionable to society or to the individual. Chapter 10 described personality disorders especially antisocial personality disorders characterized by lack of guilt. Chapter 11 covered substance abuse.

Chapters 12 and 13 deal with sexual problems. Chapter 12 focused on psychosexual disorders involving socially objectionable sexual behaviors. In many cases the individuals involved share society's disapproval of the behaviors but feel a compulsive urge to engage in them anyway.

Chapter 13 will discuss sexual dysfunctions in which people wish to enjoy normal sexual activities but are inhibited in doing so. These problems are similar to those covered earlier in that they involve specific sexual behaviors. They differ in that they are primarily objectionable to the individual experiencing the problem. Sexual dysfunctions limit the sufferer's ability to participate fully in intimate relations. They result in frustrations and misunderstandings that can destroy the most rewarding of relations.

Chapter 13 finishes the text's discussion of social problems. Chapter 14 will discuss schizophrenia. The bizarre, disorganized behaviors of schizophrenics have been the source of much research and theoretical interest over the years. Despite this effort, our knowledge of the causes and treatment of schizophrenia remains distinctly limited. In fact, disagreement continues even over how to describe and understand the problem.

CHAPTER SUMMARY

Chapter 13 begins by explaining the sexual response cycle. This provides a basis for discussing ways in which the cycle can be disrupted and theories of how the disruptions occur.

The Sexual Response Cycle begins with the initial desire for sex and includes; arousal or excitement, plateau, orgasm, and resolution. Inhibitions due to a variety of factors may disrupt an individual in one or more of these phases. Most people normally experience these disruptions from time to time. The disruptions are considered sexual dysfunctions only if they are persistent and disturbing problems.

The Sexual Dysfunctions: Descriptions and Causes describes dysfunctions as difficulties in stages of the sexual response cycle. While organic factors may be involved, psychological factors are usually central. Theories of Psychosexual Dysfunctions: General Considerations summarizes Masters and Johnson's view that historical factors (including attitudes toward sex, unfavorable early experiences, and lack of sexual information and skills) may lead the individual to develop performance fears or adopt a spectator role thus inhibiting full participation in sexual activities.

Behavioral and Cognitve Therapies for Psychosexual Dysfunctions focus both on sexual skills and on the relationship. Methods include providing information, exploring attitudes, and providing new sexual skills and experiences. Medical procedures are included where appropriate. Preliminary data suggest that these procedures may be quite effective in relieving the suffering of individuals with sexual dysfunctions.

STUDY OBJECTIVES

After studying Chapter 13 you should know

1. Master's and Johnson's description of the sexual response cycle including the excitement phase, the plateau phase, the orgasmic phase, and the resolution phase.

2. That sexual dysfunctions represent disturbances in one or more phases of the sexual response cycle.

3. the various sexual dysfunctions including inhibited sexual desire, inhibited sexual excitement, inhibited female orgasm, premature ejaculation, functional vaginismus, and functional dyspareunia.

4. That Masters and Johnson assert that fears about performance and the spectator role are current factors that can cause sexual dysfunctions.

5. That religious orthodoxy, psychosexual trauma, inadequate education, and physiological causes are among the historical factors related to sexual dysfunctions.

6. That Masters and Johnson have developed effective treatments for sexual dysfunctions including anxiety reduction, education, frank discussion about sexuality, and techniques for treating various sexual dysfunctions.

KEY TERMS

Psychosexual dysfunctions (p. 314)

Sexual response cycle (p. 314)

Excitement phase (p. 315)

Plateau phase (p. 315)

Orgasmic phase (p. 315)

Resolution phase (p. 315)

Refractory period (p. 315)

Inhibited sexual desire (p. 318)

Inhibited sexual excitement (p. 319)

Inhibited female orgasm (p. 319)

Inhibited male orgasm (p. 320)

Premature ejaculation (p. 320)

Functional vaginismus (p. 321)

Functional dyspareunia (p. 321)

Spectator role (p. 323)

Fears about performance (p. 323)

In vivo desensitization (p. 326)

Sensory-awareness procedures (p. 327)

STUDY QUESTIONS

1. In general, what are "psychosexual dysfunctions"? How do they differ from the sexual disorders discussed in the previous chapter? (p. 314)

THE SEXUAL RESPONSE CYCLE (p. 314 - 318)

2. Summarize Masters and Johnson's four phases of the sexual response cycle and a factor they overlooked. Why was their work important? (p. 314 - 316)

THE SEXUAL DYSFUNCTIONS: DESCRIPTIONS AND CAUSES (p. 318 - 321)

3. At what point should people begin to think of themselves as being sexually dysfunctional? Why should you be cautious about believing everything the text will say about causes of dysfunctions? (p. 318)

4. Seven sexual dysfunctions are discussed in the text. For each summarize, (1) the definition, (2) any problems with the definition, and (3) possible causes of the problem. (p. 318 - 321)

THEORIES OF PSYCHOSEXUAL DYSFUNCTIONS: GENERAL CONSIDERATIONS (p. 321 - 326)

5. According to Masters and Johnson, how do current and historical factors interact to result in sexual dysfunctions? Briefly describe their two current and eight historical factors. (p. 323 - 325)

6. Summarize five additional points that have come from other contemporary views of sexual dysfunctions. (p. 325 - 326)

BEHAVIORAL AND COGNITIVE THERAPIES FOR PSYCHOSEXUAL DYSFUNCTIONS (p. 326 - 330)

7. How effective are behavioral and cognitive therapies for sexual dysfunctions? (p. 326)

8. Briefly describe eight techniques used in treating sexual dysfunctions. Notice that, in practice, combinations of these techniques are used. (p. 326 - 330)

SELF-TEST, CHAPTER 13

MULTIPLE-CHOICE

1. Psychosexual dysfunctions are best described as
   A. Bizarre sexual behaviors
   B. Indirect indicators of more serious underlying psychological disorders
   C. Inhibitions in normal sexual response patterns
   D. Immature or impulsive sexual misbehaviors

2. In the "excitement phase" of the sexual response cycle individuals
   A. First decide to begin sexual activity
   B. Are initially aroused by sexual stimulation
   C. Experience gradually increasing levels of sexual tension
   D. Experience a peak level of sexual arousal

3. According to Masters & Johnson
   A. Most women object to intercourse during menstruation
   B. Most women experience more intense orgasms from large penises
   C. Simultaneous orgasms are not especially desirable
   D. Intercourse should be avoided during pregnancy

4. Which of the following dysfunctions is most difficult to define in purely objective or physical terms?
   A. Inhibited sexual desire
   B. Inhibited sexual excitement
   C. Functional vaginismus
   D. Functional dyspareunia

5. In bioenergetic treatment for sexual dysfunctions the patient
   A. Receives physical therapy to relieve muscle tension
   B. Is urged to face the childhood origins of the dysfunction
   C. Carries out sexual activities with a partner
   D. Is trained in biofeedback techniques for relieving anxiety

6. Most contemporary therapies for sexual dysfunctions utilize a ___________ approach

   A. Psychoanalytic
   B. Social-learning
   C. Humanistic
   D. Physiological

7. Which of the following is defined as a currently relevant factor in sexual dysfunctions by Masters & Johnson?

   A. Religious orthodoxy
   B. Psychosexual trauma
   C. Spectator roles
   D. Excessive intake of alcohol

8. Other contemporary sex therapists have emphasized the role of ___________ in sexual dysfunctions

   A. Hormonal factors
   B. Pornographic overstimulation
   C. Poor communication between partners
   D. All of the above

9. Psychological methods of treating sexual dysfunctions

   A. Appear to be quite successful generally
   B. Have been developed for roughly half the known dysfunctions
   C. Have been more successful in treating females than males
   D. Are so new that little information is available

10. Therapy for sexually dysfunctional couples often emphasizes helping the couple

   A. Focus on vaginal, not clitoral, stimulation
   B. Achieve simultaneous orgasms
   C. Understand the intrapsychic causes of their problems
   D. Become more aware of sexual sensations

SHORT ANSWER

1. List, in order, the four stages of the sexual response cycle as described by Masters & Johnson.

2. Most modern sexologists agree that female orgasms are evoked by stimulation of ____________.

3. At what point should a person be considered to have a sexual dysfunction according to DSM-III?

4. The DSM-III label ____________ refers to problems of impotence and frigidity.

5. Define "functional vaginismus".

6. What sexually dysfunctional behavior is most often the result of physical factors?

7. List the seven or eight historical factors leading to sexual dysfunction according to Masters & Johnson.

8. Why do spectator roles and performance fears make sexual intercourse difficult?

9. List a number of components of therapy for sexual dysfunctions which do NOT focus directly on sexual activity as such.

10. Describe "sensate focusing" as a component of sexual therapy.

ANSWERS TO SELF-TEST, CHAPTER 13

MULTIPLE-CHOICE

1. C (p. 314)
2. B (p. 315)
3. C (p. 316-317)
4. A (p. 318-319)
5. A (p. 322)
6. B (p. 323)
7. C (p. 324)
8. C (p. 325-326)
9. A (p. 326)
10. D (p. 327)

SHORT ANSWER

1. Excitement phase, Plateau phase, Orgasmic phase, Resolution phase. (p. 315)

2. Clitoris. (p. 316-317)

3. When the behavior becomes "recurrent and persistent". Occasional disturbances are considered normal. (p. 318)

4. Inhibited sexual excitement. (p. 319)

5. Involuntary contractions of the vagina when insertion is attempted. (p. 321)

6. Dyspareunia or pain during intercourse. (p. 321)

7. Religious orthodoxy, Psychosexual trauma, Homosexual inclination, Inadequate counseling, Extensive alcohol intake, Vaginismus, Physiological causes, Sociocultural factors. (p. 323-324)

8. They distract or divert the individual's attention away from sexual stimulation & enjoyment. (p. 323)

9. Sex education, anxiety reduction, skills & communication training, Shifts in routine, marital & other therapy, etc. (p. 326-327)

10. Couple undress and practice giving (and receiving) pleasure by touching and caressing each other. (p. 328-329)

14 Schizophrenia

OVERVIEW

Chapter 13 discussed sexual dysfunctions and was the last of four chapters on social problems characterized by socially disapproved behaviors and personality patterns.

Chapter 14 discusses schizophrenia. Of all the disorders covered in the text, schizophrenia comes closest to the common understanding of "madness" or "insanity". Despite extensive study, it remains a major concern both socially and scientifically. Historically schizophrenia has been a major problem, accounting for about half of all hospitalized mental patients. Today efforts are made to get schizophrenics out of institutions - but follow-up community treatment has proven difficult.

Scientifically, schizophrenia has also been a problem. Historically, psychologists have disagreed on how to define schizophrenia and even on whether the term refers to one or to several different problems. Not surprisingly, the result has been widespread differences in theoretical approaches, research orientations, and diagnostic practices.

After Chapter 14 the next section of the text deals with developmental disorders. Developmental disorders cover the range of problems people may develop in the processes of growing up, facing adulthood, and growing old. These disorders include problems often first seen in children, including mental retardation.

CHAPTER SUMMARY

The <u>History of the Concept</u> of schizophrenia has included two traditions. Many American ideas about schizophrenia developed out of Bleuler's broad, psychoanalytically based, definition. DSM-III has moved toward Kraepelin's narrower, descriptive (rather than theoretical), approach which has been popular in Europe.

<u>Clinical Symptoms of Schizophrenia</u> are divided into five areas. Thought problems include both the content or ideas expressed and the form or manner in which the schizophrenia thinks. Disorders of perception and attention include unrealistic delusions (thoughts) and hallucinations (sensory experiences). Peculiar motor and affective symptoms, and distinctive impairments in life functioning are common.

DSM-III recognizes three <u>Subcatagories of Schizophrenia.</u> Disorganized schizophrenics exhibit blatantly bizarre and silly behaviors. Catatonic schizophrenics show primarily motor symptoms including wild excitement and apathetic withdrawal to the point of immobility. Paranoid schizophrenics have organized delusions of persecution, grandiosity, and jealousy.

<u>Research on the Etiology of Schizophrenia</u> has been extensive. Schizophrenics are typically impoverished and come from confused families with ineffective, confused relationships and communications. It is unclear whether schizophrenia results from, or is a cause of, these social and family conditions.

Genetic data from family, twin, and more sophisticated adoptee studies all point to a genetic predisposition to schizophrenia. Research on the possible physiological factors involved is difficult and confusing. Drug studies using schizophrenics suggest excessive activity in nerve tracts of the brain that utilize the neurotransmitter dopamine. New neurological techniques suggest brain atrophy in some schizophrenics leading to speculation that different physiological factors may be involved for these individuals.

Since schizophrenia runs in families it possible to select and follow children with a high risk of becoming schizophrenic. These studies suggest several factors which differ for males and females.

Many physical and psychological Therapies for Schizophrenia have been attempted. Many physical methods such as electroshock largely disappeared with the development of antipsychotic drugs, especially the phenothiazines. Drugs were a major advance that allowed the current emphasis on getting and keeping schizophrenics out of institutions. However schizophrenics need additional help to cope with social living and resolve their possible inner problems. Ego-analysts try to form close relationships with schizophrenics so the schizophrenic can feel secure enough to explore repressed childhood traumas. The effectiveness of this method is unclear. Behavioral approaches try to train social skills so that schizophrenics can better cope with society or institutional life.

STUDY OBJECTIVES

After studying Chapter 14 you should know:

1. The history of the diagnosis of schizophrenia including Kraepelin's dementia praecox, Bleuler's associative threads, and the broadened American concepts such as the process-reactive distinction.

2. The major symptoms of schizophrenia -- disordered thought, disorders of perception and attention, motor behavior, affective abnormalities, and problems in life functioning.

3. The three major subcategories of schizophrenia -- disorganized, catatonic, and paranoid.

4. The new distinction between positive symptoms (hallucinations, delusions, bizarre behavior) and negative symptoms (flat affect, language deficits, apathy, anhedonia, and attentional impairment).

5. That those broad theoretical views that have been offered about the etiology of schizophrenia have generated little research and are of dubious value.

6. That there is a link between lower social class status and schizophrenia, and that social drift and social stress explanations both appear to be partially accurate interpretations of this correlation.

7. That there is little strong evidence that the family plays an important etiological role in schizophrenia, although recent data suggest that family emotional expression may be related to subsequent relapse.

8. That evidence from family, twin, and adoption studies indicates that there is a substantial genetic contribution to schizophrenia, although genetics cannot fully explain the disorder's etiology.

9. That recent biological evidence suggests that excess dopamine activity and brain pathology appear to be related to symptoms in some subsets of schizophrenic patients.

10. That children of schizophrenic patients are being studied longitudinally in a number of high-risk projects which may shed light on the etiology of schizophrenia.

11. That there is little evidence that psychotherapy alone is an effective treatment for schizophrenia.

12. That neuroleptic medications have a dramatically beneficial effect in quieting the symptoms of schizophrenia.

13. That social learning therapy is the most effective of the psychological treatments for mental patients since it teaches coping skills that allow for greater independence.

KEY TERMS

Schizophrenia (p. 334)

Dementia praecox (p. 334)

Process-reactive (p. 336)

Schizoaffective disorder (p. 337)

Schizophreniform disorder (p. 337)

Thought disorder (p. 338)

Incoherence (p. 338)

Neologism (p. 338)

Loose associations (p. 338)

Clang associations (p. 338)

Poverty of speech or content (p. 338)

Perseveration (p. 338)

Blocking (p. 338)

Lack of insight (p. 338)

Delusions (p. 338)

Hallucinations (p. 341)

Catatonic immobility (p. 341)

Waxy flexibility (p. 341)

Flat and inappropriate affect (p. 341 - 342)

Disorganized (or hebephrenic) schizophrenia (p. 342)

Catatonic schizophrenia (p. 342)

Paranoid schizophrenia (p. 343)

Grandiose delusions (p. 343)

Delusional jealousy (p. 343)

Ideas of reference (p. 343)

Positive (& negative) symptoms (p. 343)

Sociogenic hypothesis (p. 341)

Social-drift theory (p. 341)

Schizophrenic mother (p. 342)

Double bind hypothesis (p. 342)

Phenothiazines (p. 355)

Dopamine theory (p. 355)

High-risk method (p. 358)

Insulin coma therapy (p. 360

Prefrontal lobotomy (p. 360)

Neuroleptics (p. 360)

Chlorpromazine (p. 360)

Direct analysis (p. 361)

STUDY QUESTIONS

HISTORY OF THE CONCEPT (p. 335 - 337)

1. Describe Kraepelin's and Bleuler's early views on schizophrenia. Trace the way Bleuler's broader view developed in America. (p. 335 - 337)

2. List four ways in which the DSM-III definition of schizophrenia has moved toward the narrower European definition. (p. 337)

CLINICAL SYMPTOMS OF SCHIZOPHRENIA (p. 337 - 342)

3. Schizophrenics may display disturbances in five areas. Are disturbances typically present in all five? Briefly describe the five areas. (p. 337 - 342)

SUBCATAGORIES OF SCHIZOPHRENIA (p. 342 - 344)

4. Summarize the one or two major characteristics of each of three subcategories of schizophrenia in DSM-III. (p. 342 - 343)

5. Briefly explain the limitations of the DSM-III subcatagories. What other distinction does the text propose? (p. 343 - 344)

RESEARCH ON THE ETIOLOGY OF SCHIZOPHRENIA (p. 344 - 360)

6. What relationship has been found between social class and schizophrenia? What two explanations can be offered for these results? (p. 344 - 348)

7. Briefly define two early views on the role of the family; i.e. the schizophrenogenic mother and the double-bind. Describe the possible roles of the family in causing or maintaining schizophrenia according to more recent research. (p. 348 - 350)

8. Describe three methods of studying genetic factors in schizophrenia. How have the first two methods been criticized and how does the third method attempt to answer the criticism? (p. 350 - 354)

9. What conclusions do the authors reach regarding genetic factors in schizophrenia? What model do they feel is most appropriate? (p. 354)

10. Why do the results of genetic studies suggest that biochemical factors may be important in schizophrenia? Why have these biochemical factors been hard to study? (p. 354)

11. What two biochemical factors were suggested by early research? Explain each briefly. (p. 354)

12. Explain the theory of excess dopamine activity. What kinds of data support this theory and what data suggests it is limited? (p. 354 - 357)

13. Summarize recent neurological findings regarding schizophrenics. What does this suggest about the excessive dopamine theory? (p. 357 - 358)

14. What are the advantages of high-risk studies of schizophrenia? In general what have these studies found? (p. 358 - 360)

THERAPIES FOR SCHIZOPHRENIA (p. 360 - 365)

15. Why were earlier somatic treatments abandoned? How effective are current somatic methods? (p. 360 - 361)

16. In general what approach have analysts taken in psychological treatment of schizophrenics? How effective are such insight-oriented approaches? (p. 361 - 364)

17. What have newer behavioral therapies been able to do (and not to do) in treating schizophrenia? Why are these approaches important? (p. 364 - 365)

SELF-TEST, CHAPTER 14

MULTIPLE-CHOICE

1. DSM-III narrowed the definition of schizophrenia by including all BUT which one of the following
   - A. Requires symptoms for at least six months
   - B. Provides more explicit detailed criteria
   - C. Excludes patients with affective symptoms
   - D. Considers family history of schizophrenia

2. "Disorder of thought form" means that many schizophrenics
   - A. Organize their ideas poorly
   - B. Have bizarre delusional ideas
   - C. Lack insight into their behavior
   - D. See things that are not really there

3. In addition to specific symptoms schizophrenics manifest impairments in their life functioning including
   - A. Difficulty making friends
   - B. Poor bowel and bladder control
   - C. Hostile acting out behaviors
   - D. Difficulty controlling sexual urges

4. Some schizophrenics experience virtually no emotional response even in situations that most people would find very happy, sad, etc. This is called
   - A. Blocking
   - B. Neologism
   - C. Hebephrenia
   - D. Flat affect

5. A prominent symptom of catatonic schizophrenics is that they
   - A. Are convinced they are almost perfect and are persecuted because others are jealous
   - B. Giggle childishly and talk complete nonsense
   - C. Remain immobile in unusual positions for long periods
   - D. Attack others without provocation

6. A major problem in studying the relationship between social class and schizophrenia is that
   - A. Lower class schizophrenics who cannot afford hospital care are not detected
   - B. Hospitals are limited in providing records due to legal requirements
   - C. People who go into the community to make ratings are poorly trained
   - D. People move frequently making follow-up measurement difficult

7. Research indicates that most schizophrenics come from
   - A. Single parent families
   - B. Families with a schizophrenic parent
   - C. Educated and prosperous families
   - D. Rural families

8. The best evidence of a genetic component in schizophrenia comes from studies of
   - A. Ancestors of known schizophrenics
   - B. Twins of known schizophrenics
   - C. Schizophrenics who were adopted at a young age
   - D. Schizophrenics who are unable to have children

9. The role of excess dopamine activity in schizophrenia should be considered cautiously because
   - A. Recent studies indicate some schizophrenics do not have dopamine
   - B. Dopamine may also play a role in amphetamine psychosis
   - C. Other research suggests that genetic factors are important
   - D. Research in such areas is often contradicted later

10. Which of the following is currently most used in treating schizophrenia?
   - A. Insulin coma therapy
   - B. Prefrontal lobotomy
   - C. Antipsychotic drugs
   - D. Existential psychotherapy

11. Behavioral therapies for schizophrenia attempt to teach
    A. Improved social skills
    B. Better patterns of thinking
    C. Appropriate responses to double-bind communication
    D. Attending to outside stimuli

SHORT ANSWER

1. What characteristics of the problem were emphasized by A) Kraepelin's term "dementia praecox" and B) Bleuler's term "schizophrenia"?

2. "Reactive schizophrenics" (as opposed to "process schizophrenics" were characterized by . . .

3. What characteristic of schizophrenic speech is illustrated by each of the following.
    A. "I feel fine, on the line, just my kind."

    B. "I'm all frammeled out with psychobabbelology."

    C. "His pants were blue as the sky with clouds floating across it, all fluffy like pink cotton candy that tastes like strawberries."

4. A "delusion" is a ____________ while a hallucination is a ____________.

5. Why is there much interest in positive and negative symptoms of schizophrenia?

6. Briefly discuss the importance of genetic factors in the development of schizophrenia.

7. In what way does the effect of phenothiazines suggest that dopamine is involved in schizophrenia?

8. What do recent neurological findings suggest about the brains of schizophrenics?

9. Describe the research procedures used in "high-risk" studies of schizophrenia.

10. How effective is traditional insight-oriented psychotherapy in treating schizophrenia? Explain briefly.

ANSWERS TO SELF-TEST, CHAPTER 14

MULTIPLE-CHOICE

1. D (p. 337)	2. A (p. 338)	3. A (p. 342)
4. D (p. 341)	5. C (p. 342-343)	6. C (p. 348)
7. B (p. 348-350)	8. C (p. 352-353)	9. D (p. 357)
10. C (p. 360)	11. A (p. 364)	

SHORT ANSWER

1. A) Early onset and progressive intellectual deterioration B) Underlying difficulty in efficient thinking & communication. (p. 334-335)

2. Good functioning prior to the problem, rapid onset of problem possibly late in life, good prognosis for recovery. (p. 336)

3. A. Clang associations. B) neologisms. C) Loose associations. (p. 338)

4. Distorted thought, distorted perception. (p. 338,341)

5. Continued search for better ways to describe schizophrenic characteristics. Traditional ways to sub-catagorize schizophrenics have proven limited. (p. 343)

6. Although earlier studies were flawed, recent studies suggest that genetic factors predispose individuals to develop schizophrenia under certain conditions. The nature of this relationship remains unclear. (p. 354)

7. Phenothiazines, which alleviate schizophrenic symptoms, produce side effects resembling Parkinson's which is caused by low dopamine. They also control amphetamine psychoses. (p. 355)

8. Brain damage may exist in some schizophrenics - especially chronic schizophrenics with negative symptoms. (p. 357-358)

9. Children of schizophrenic mothers are intensively studied as they grow up. Later those who develop schizophrenia are compared to those who do not. (p. 358-360)

10. Not very effective. Schizophrenics have difficulty relating to therapists and using insights to change. The few studies reporting improvements have been flawed in various ways. (p. 362-364)

15 Specific Disorders of Childhood and Adolescence

OVERVIEW

Chapter 14 completed the discussion of schizophrenia.

Chapter 15 begins three chapters covering developmental disorders. These include not only problems of childhood and growing up but also problems of the elderly and growing old. In some cases these disorders are specifically linked to developmental variables. In others, the disorders are usually first noticed at certain ages and the causes are more varied or are unknown.

Chapter 15 discusses a wide variety of disorders which occur in childhood. Two more childhood disorders, mental retardation and childhood psychosis, are reserved for Chapter 16. Childhood disorders cover a wide range of problems. This reflects increased recognition of the wide variety of problems children and adolescents may experience.

Chapter 17 concludes the section by discussing disorders of the elderly. This chapter reflects growing recognition of the particular psychological needs and problems of older people.

CHAPTER SUMMARY

The section on Classification points out that professionals, and DSM-III, are realizing that children develop a wide range of problems. The chapter is organized around four kinds of problems. Specific developmental disorders or Learning Disabilities are developmental delays in specific areas (reading, etc.) not related to general intellectual retardation. These disorders are usually attributed either to perceptual deficits or faulty teaching. Treatment consists of trying to teach the missing specific skills. Enuresis or bedwetting is treated similarly.

Disorders of Undercontrolled Behavior include attention deficit disorders and conduct disorders. Children with attention deficit disorders have trouble focusing their attention and are often hyperactive. Findings in a number of areas suggest a physiological basis for hyperactivity although other data suggest that parents at least exacerbate the problem. Treatment combines drugs with behavioral rewards for desire behavior. Conduct disorders are similar to juvenile delinquency and are linked to a variety of factors including genetic deficits, family conflict, and role models provided by parents or friends. Treatment programs reward social behavior and teach academic skills.

In Disorders of Overcontrolled Behavior, fears and worries lead to problems such as school phobia, withdrawal and depression. School phobia may be better thought of as fear of separation from parents. Gradual exposure to school and rewards for attendance prove effective. Other overcontrol problems are often not recognized and are poorly understood. Play therapy and family therapy are common forms of treatment.

Two Eating Disorders are recognized. Anorexia nervosa involves inadequate food intake so that the victim, usually female, may starve to death. There is little support for the many theories of anorexia and treatment, usually including family therapy, is difficult. In bulimia the individual gorges herself them purges the food by vomiting or using laxatives. Although not life-threatening, bulimia can also have serious physical consequences.

STUDY OBJECTIVES

After studying Chapter 15 you should know:

1. That childhood disorders have been understudied compared to adult psychopathology although DSM-III includes a more detailed -- and controversial -- listing of childhood disorders than existed in previous manuals, .

2. That overcontrol and undercontrol are two broad dimensions of childhood disorders that are consistently identified.

3. That learning disabilities are specific developmental disorders, problems in an isolated area of academic functioning.

4. That hyperactivity and conduct disorders are the two major subcategories of conduct disorders.

5. That Attention Deficit Disorder with Hyperactivity is a problem which probably has multiple causes and is characterized by inattention, impulsivity, overactivity, academic difficulties, and troubled peer relationships.

6. That conduct disorders are defined by the child's impact on the environment, and tend to be long-lasting difficulties that can be resistive to treatment.

7. That overcontrolled behavior disorders (e.g. fears, social withdrawal, and depression) are defined by their negative impact on the child rather than the environment.

8. The difference between anorexia nervosa (a dramatic,often life-threatening loss of weight) and bulimia (binge-eating and self-induced vomiting), both of which are more common among females.

KEY TERMS

Specific developmental disorders
(or learning disabilities) (p. 372)

Dyslexia (p. 372)

Perceptual-deficit theory (p. 373)

Academic-instruction theory (p. 373)

Disorders of undercontrolled behavior (p. 374)

Attention deficit disorder with hyperactivity (p. 375)

Conduct disorders (p. 380)

Socialized (& unsocialized) conduct disorders (p. 380)

Coercion hypothesis (p. 384)

Disorders of overcontrolled behavior (p. 386)

School phobia (p. 388)

Social withdrawal (p. 389)

Elective mutism (p. 389)

Anorexia nervosa (p. 391)

Bulimia (p. 396)

STUDY QUESTIONS

CLASSIFICATION (p. 370 - 372)

1. How does DSM-III differ from earlier DSM's in it's approach to classifying childhood problems? Why is it important to remember that problem children are identified by others not themselves? (p. 370 - 372)

LEARNING DISABILITIES (p. 372 - 374)

2. Define specific developmental disorders (or learning disabilities) and give several examples. (p. 372)

3. Briefly describe two current views on the causes of learning disabilities. What kind of intervention is commonly used? (p. 373 - 374)

DISORDERS OF UNDERCONTROLLED BEHAVIOR (p. 374 - 386)

4. How does the label "attention deficit disorder" change the way we think about hyperactivity? Distinguish between hyperactivity and "just an active kid". (p. 374 - 378)

5. Why is any one theory not likely to explain all hyperactivity? Briefly describe four physiological and two psychological theories of hyperactivity. (p. 378 - 379)

6. Evaluate the effectiveness of two somatic and one behavioral treatment for hyperactivity. (p. 379 - 380)

7. Describe two types of conduct disorders. Why does the impact of a child's behavior on others make it difficult to clearly define conduct disorders? (p. 380 - 382)

8. What evidence exists for physiological explanations of conduct disorders? Summarize the psychological theories pointing out how they all point to similar factors. (p. 382 - 384)

9. Why is treatment of conduct disorders important - and difficult? Evaluate the effectiveness of two behavioral approaches. (p. 384 - 386)

DISORDERS OF OVERCONTROLLED BEHAVIOR (p. 386 - 391)

10. Summarize our understandings of the development of childhood fears, school phobias, and social withdrawal. Identify three behavioral principles used in treating these fears. (p. 386 - 390)

11. Explain the controversies about the frequency and definition of affective disorders in childhood. (p. 390 - 391)

EATING DISORDERS (p. 391 - 398)

12. Define anorexia nervosa and bulimia noting other symptoms associated with them. Summarize the two steps in treating anorexia nervosa. (p. 391 - 398)

SELF-TEST, CHAPTER 15

MULTIPLE-CHOICE

1. Which of the following is a major problem in understanding and treating childhood disorders
   A. Adult professionals have difficulty understanding the child's perspective
   B. Most problems are variable and soon outgrown
   C. Children are referred for treatment by adults
   D. There are few personality tests for children

2. Treatment of specific learning disabilities typically involves
   A. Teaching academic skills
   B. A high-protein, low-salt diet
   C. Drug treatment of neurological deficits
   D. Training improved social skills

3. The DSM-III definition focuses on the idea that hyperactivity is a result of
   A. Delayed development of social skills
   B. Minimal brain damage
   C. Excessive academic pressures
   D. Inability to concentrate on tasks

4. A child who misbehaves may be defined as having a conduct disorder depending on whether
   A. Parents & teachers consider the problem serious
   B. The behavior is illegal
   C. The child misbehaves alone or with others
   D. Neurological symptoms are also present

5. Several theories suggest that conduct disorders develop in children from families that
   A. Have many children
   B. Are overprotective
   C. Emphasize physical punishment
   D. Induce anxiety and guilt

6. Apparently successful programs for treating conduct disorders emphasize
   - A. Teaching academic and social skills
   - B. Strenuous exercise and contact sports
   - C. Placing strict contingencies on misbehavior
   - D. Developing close relationships with police officers who volunteer their time

7. Parents should take their children's fears seriously because such fears
   - A. Often develop into adult problems
   - B. Frequently reflect other deeper problems
   - C. Are difficult to treat
   - D. Can be especially traumatic for children

8. There is most controversy over the definition and symptoms of
   - A. Learning disabilities
   - B. Hyperactivity
   - C. Affective disorders of childhood
   - D. Eating disorders

9. Which of the following distinguishes anorexia nervosa from bulimia
   - A. Depression
   - B. Pronounced weight loss
   - C. Overconcern with food and dieting
   - D. Occurs primarily among women

10. Which of the following is NOT characteristic of individuals with bulimia?
   - A. They often have behavior problems in school
   - B. They are often depressed
   - C. They have physiological problems as a result of bulimia
   - D. Their eating behavior is similar to many normal dieters

SHORT ANSWER

1. Over the years what changes have occurred in classification systems for childhood disorders?

2. Define "specific developmental disorders".

3. Identify the two major views on psychological factors in learning disabilities.

4. Summarize the research on brain damage as a cause of hyperactivity.

5. How effective are somatic treatments for hyperactivity?

6. Distinguish between undersocialized and socialized conduct disorder.

7. "School phobia" is best understood, not as fear of school, but as fear of . . .

8. Identify several procedures used in helping children overcome childhood fears and social withdrawl.

9. Describe the assumptions behind the "family lunch session" as a treatment for anorexia.

10. What is known about the causes of anorexia and bulimia?

ANSWERS TO SELF-TEST, CHAPTER 15

MULTIPLE-CHOICE

1. C (p. 372)
2. A (p. 373-374)
3. D (p. 375)
4. A (p. 380)
5. C (p. 384)
6. A (p. 385)
7. D (p. 387-388)
8. C (p. 390)
9. B (p. 396)
10. A (p. 396-397)

SHORT ANSWER

1. They have expanded and changed radically becoming more sophisticated. Earlier systems were simple downward extensions of adult disorders. (p. 370)

2. Learning disabilities or deficits in development of specific intellectual skills such as reading, arithmetic, language and speech. (p. 372-373)

3. Deficits in perception of stimuli, poor teaching and education. (p. 373)

4. Several lines of research indirectly suggest the possibility but no specific kinds of brain damage have been shown to be involved. (p. 378-379)

5. Drugs reduce behavior problems but have little effect on (and may harm) academic achievement. Diet has little effect on most hyperactive children. (p. 379-380)

6. Distinction is whether the individual misbehaves with peers (socialized) or has few friends and misbehaves alone. (p. 380)

7. Separation from home and parents. (p. 388-389)

8. Expose child to feared situation while providing encouragement and reinforcement. Provide models and teach skills for appropriate behavior. (p. 389-390)

9. Assumes that not eating deflects attention away from family conflicts thus keeping the family together. (p. 396)

10. Very little. Many speculations have been offered but none are supported. (p. 393-394,398)

16 Mental Retardation and Infantile Autism

OVERVIEW

Chapter 16 is the second of three chapters devoted to developmental disorders. The previous chapter covered childhood problems which were relatively specific. Each topic referred to problem behaviors which were relatively clearcut. Chapter 16 will cover two additional problems of childhood which are relatively broader and have more serious implications for a child's overall development and functioning.

The next chapter (Chapter 17) will deal with problems of aging. Older individual are subject to a wide variety of problems. They must cope with the physical problems of aging. More importantly they must cope with the realization that they are getting older as well as the fact that society often does not seem to respect, value, or provide for them.

CHAPTER SUMMARY

Chapter 16 covers two problems. A diagnosis of Mental Retardation involves three criteria; subnormal intellectual functioning, deficits in adaptive behavior, and onset before age 18. Severe retardation usually results from physical factors including chromosomal abnormalities, diseases, malnutrition, or brain injuries.

Milder retardation is much more common and is the center of much social and scientific interest. Social and environmental factors are considered the primary causes. Special educational and social enrichment programs seek to prevent or minimize retardation, particularly under provisions of Public Law 94-142. Educational and behavioral programs are used to treat problems of retarded individuals as well as improve their intellectual functioning.

Chapter 16 also discusses Early Infantile Autism. This is, fortunately, an uncommon disorder in which very young children show profound problems in speech, learning, and social relations. Research has not supported early theories which suggested that autistic children had been rejected by emotionally cold parents. Possible physiological causes are suggested by the problem's early onset, by family and twin studies, by research indicating EEG and neurological abnormalities, and by the disorder's similarity to some physical syndromes.

Treatments for autism have focused on behavioral procedures using modeling and operant conditioning and on fenfluramine; a drug which seems to reduce some symptoms. However most autistic children remain intellectually and socially limited.

STUDY OBJECTIVES

After studying Chapter 16 you should know:

1. The diagnostic criteria for mental retardation: (a) significantly subaverage intellectual functioning; (b) deficits in adaptive behavior; and (c) onset during the developmental period.

2. The classification levels of mental retardation (mild, moderate, severe, and profound), the IQ cutoff scores associated with each level, and the prognosis for members of each level.

3. That the specific etiology for most cases of mental retardation is unknown (cultural-familial deprivation and undetected brain impairments are suggested), and that these cases generally fall in the mild category.

4. About the known causes of mental retardation including Down's Syndrome, PKU, infectious causes, and fetal alcohol syndrome.

5. That early interventions such as Project Head Start can lead to improvements in intellectual functioning but that, once the intervention is withdrawn, regression is common.

6. About the deinstitutionalization movement and Public Law 94-142, both of which have radically changed the way the retarded are treated in our society.

7. That infantile autism is characterized by extreme autistic aloneness, severely limited language, and ritualistic behavior.

8. That most autistic children (80%) score in the retarded range on IQ tests.

9. That the specific etiology of infantile autism remains unknown, although some sort of physiological, rather that psychological, factor is almost certainly the cause.

10. That highly structured social-learning treatments have been successful in reducing self-injury and in improving communication and self-care skills among autistic children.

11. That a new medication, Fenfluramine, appears to help improve the autistic child's behavior and ability to learn, although the drug is far from a cure for this disorder.

KEY TERMS

Mental retardation (p. 400)

Down's syndrome (p. 408)

Phenylketonuria (p. 409)

Tay-Sachs disease (p. 409

Fetal alcohol syndrome (p. 412)

Deinstitutionalization (p. 416)

Public Law 94-142 (p. 416)

Infantile autism (p. 420)

Echolalia (p. 423)

Pronoun reversal (p. 423)

Time-out procedure (p. 428)

STUDY QUESTIONS

MENTAL RETARDATION (p. 400 - 420)

1. Define "mental retardation" using DSM-III's three criteria. Describe how psychologists decide if someone meets the first two criteria. (p. 400 - 402)

2. DSM-III classifies four intellectual degrees of retardation. For each, give (1) the IQ range, (2) the expected degree of social adaptation, and (3) common causes of the problem. (p. 402 - 403)

3. Describe the kinds of deficiencies retarded individuals may have in six adaptive skill areas (p. 403 - 405)

4. Explain why it is frequently inappropriate to describe degree of retardation using age levels. Briefly describe four areas of research into the general cognitive abilities of retarded individuals. (p. 405-406)

5. Briefly describe two theories about the cause of retardation with no identifiable physical problems. Briefly describe seven organic causes of retardation. Where appropriate, describe an example of each. (p. 406 - 413)

6. Describe two approaches to prevention of mental retardation. How successful has each been? (p. 413 - 415)

7. What happened to early efforts to treat retardation? Describe current efforts by explaining four provisions of Public Law 94-142 and two psychologically based teaching strategies. (p. 415 -420)

EARLY INFANTILE AUTISM (p. 420 - 429)

8. Describe infantile autism in general and it's relation to retardation. Describe three characteristic deficits in autism and the prognosis for autistic children. (p. 420 - 424)

9. Summarize early psychological theories of autism including the ideas of hopelessness, shutting out the world, and parental roles. How well has research supported these theories? (p. 424 - 425)

10. Describe two research areas suggesting a physiological basis for infantile autism. (p. 426)

11. Why are autistic children especially difficult to treat? Summarize four approaches to treating autism (p. 426 -429)

SELF-TEST, CHAPTER 16

MULTIPLE-CHOICE

1. What DSM III label is appropriate for an 8 year old boy who obtains an IQ of 55 but is doing all right socially and academically
   A. Mild retardation
   B. Cultural-familial retardation
   C. Autistic
   D. None of the above

2. Individuals with IQs of 20 to 34 typically are only able to
   A. Learn basic academic skills like reading and adding
   B. Handle unskilled jobs with supervision
   C. Take case of their basic needs
   D. Make noises and walk

3. In the workplace mildly retarded people typically
   A. Are not easily distinguished from other workers
   B. Are limited to doing simple jobs for sympathetic employers
   C. Can work only in sheltered, supervised settings
   D. Are unable to perform socially valuable work

4. Which of the following is true of most retarded individuals
   A. They are moderately or severely retarded
   B. There is a known organic basis for their retardation
   C. They come from poor, socially-deprived families
   D. Their retardation is not easily identified on standard IQ tests.

5. Research on early intervention programs such as head start suggests that such programs
   A. Are ineffective in treating mental retardation
   B. Significantly decrease retardation in later years
   C. Must be continued into elementary school to be effective.
   D. Are difficult to evaluate using current methods.

6. Public Law 94-142 provides that
   A. Retarded children must be "mainstreamed" into regular classrooms whenever possible.
   B. Retarded children must receive a free education in the least restrictive environment possible.
   C. Each state must develop it's own statutes for educating retarded children
   D. The government must pay the cost of institutionalizing retarded children who cannot benefit from a normal education.

7. Which of the following best describes the relation between autism and mental retardation?
   A. Autistics are of average intelligence
   B. Autistics are untestable
   C. Autistics are clearly mentally retarded
   D. Autistics are difficult to test but probably of normal intelligence
   E. Autistics are difficult to test but probably have intellectual deficits

8. Which of the following terms refers to the fact that autistics make few demands on, and seem to ignore, others
   A. Echolalia
   B. Aloneness
   C. Pernicious
   D. Pervasive developmental disorder

9. Research indicates that ____________ autistics outgrow their childhood problems
   A. Virtually all
   B. Most
   C. Few
   D. No

10. Early psychological theories of autism proposed that parents of autistics were
   A. Overprotective
   B. Intellectually retarded
   C. Strict disciplinarians
   D. Emotionally cold

11. In the _____________ autistic acting-out behaviors are eliminated by removing the child from potentially reinforcing situations when the behavior occurs.
   A. Time out procedure
   B. Family centered approach
   C. Selective stimulation method
   D. Social punishment technique

SHORT ANSWER

1. List the three criteria for diagnosing mental retardation in DSM-III.

2. What is "Adaptive behavior" as used in defining mental retardation?

3. Briefly summarize the level of social and academic abilities expected of mildly retarded individuals.

4. Why is it often inappropriate to describe a retarded individual's deficiencies by age level (for example, saying the person "is functioning at the six-year level")?

5. What is "strategic processing" (a cognitive ability said to be deficient in retardates)?

6. Give examples of many different organic causes of retardation (the text gave six catagories).

7. ____________ was an effort to reduce the number of retarded individuals by segregating and sterilizing them.

8. Applied behavior analysis has developed methods of teaching retarded individuals to . . .

9. Define echolalia (a characteristic of autism).

10. Summarize recent research on the drug fenfluramine as a treatment for autism.

ANSWERS TO SELF-TEST, CHAPTER 16

MULTIPLE-CHOICE

1. D (p. 400-401)
2. C (p. 403)
3. A (p. 405)
4. C (p. 407)
5. C (p. 415)
6. B (p. 417-419)
7. E (p. 421-422)
8. B (p. 422)
9. C (p. 425)
10. D (p. 425)
11. A (p. 428)

SHORT ANSWER

1. A) Significantly subaverage intelligence, B) Deficits in adaptive behavior, and C) Manifest during the developmental period. (p. 400-402)

2. Adaptive behavior meets standards of personal independence and social responsibility appropriate to individual's age and culture. (p. 401)

3. As children they are not obviously different until they enter school. Academic skills usually limited to about sixth grade. As adults perform unskilled jobs and live in society but may need guidance with finances etc. (p. 403)

4. Because different skills may not develop equally. Especially social skills and interests of a retarded adult aren't often comparable to those of a child. (p. 405)

5. Strategies for thinking out and solving problems (p. 406)

6. 1) Genetic conditions such as Down's syndrome & PKU, 2) Infectious diseases effecting the pregnant mother (rubella, syphilis, etc) or child (meningitis, etc), 3) accidents & injuries, 4) Premature birth (possibly), 5) Chemical substances (thalidomide, alcohol, etc.), 6) Environmental hazards including pollutants in air, water, food, paint, etc. (p. 407-413)

7. The eugenics movement (p. 414)

8. Feed, groom, and care for themselves. To not injure themselves. (p. 419)

9. Echoing or repeating back what another person has said. (p. 423)

10. Autistics received fenfluramine or a placebo in alternation. Parents and observers, who did not know which drug was being given, rated improvement in IQ and behavior for some autistics. (p. 429)

17 Aging and Psychological Disorders

OVERVIEW

Chapter 17 is the last of three chapters on developmental disorders. The first two chapters discussed disorders of childhood and growing up. Chapter 15 covered a variety of specific developmental problems while Chapter 16 dealt with two, more pervasive, problems; mental retardation and autism. Chapter 17 is devoted to the problems of aging and growing old.

Chapter 17 completes the text's discussion of psychological disorders. The next, and last, section of the text deals more intensively with topics covered only briefly so far. Three chapters will intensively discuss treatment methods. The last chapter will cover legal and ethical issues.

CHAPTER SUMMARY

Growing old is, obviously, a time of physical decline and medical problems become an increasing concern. Beyond the purely medical aspects of old age, however, are a wide range of psychological and social problems.

The chapter begins by summarizing Concepts and Methods in the Study of Older Adults. It then gives Some Basic Facts About Older Adults including some realistic problems facing the elderly. This discussion forms a basis for considering the physical and psychological disorders of the elderly.

Brain Disorders of Old Age may be slowly developing, progressive, dementias that are usually irreversible and require supportive care. They may also be sudden deliriums that can often be reversed by treating the underlying physical conditions.

The difficulties of growing old also make the elderly especially subject to various Psychological Problems of Old Age. Depression often accompanies physical and psychological declines as people grow old. Suspiciousness and paranoia may result as the elderly experience difficulty understanding others due to hearing problems and social isolation. The elderly are also subject to other psychological problems. Suicide may result as the elderly struggle to accept changing physical and social situations.

Contrary to popular conceptions, the elderly are capable of enjoying and engaging in sexual activity despite slowed physiological responses.

The chapter concludes with a discussion of General Issues in Treatment and Care of the elderly. Nursing homes and other facilities often fail to encourage the elderly to maintain their skills and capabilities. Community-based services could help the elderly remain as independent as possible. Psychotherapy can also help the elderly accept changes and provide them support and information to continue functioning.

STUDY OBJECTIVES

After studying Chapter 17 you should know:

1. What age effects, cohort effects, and time-of-measurement effects are, and how these effects make interpretation of studies of aging difficult.

2. That the proportion of aged individuals in the population of the United States has been and will continue to grow, and that women and whites are over-represented in this population.

3. That, when interpreting data representing the aged, it is important to remember that the prevalence of chronic physical illnesses is great among the aged, poverty rates are higher than for younger age groups, housing is less adequate, prejudice exists, and many major life events (e.g. death of loved ones) have been experienced.

4. That some cognitive declines occur with increasing age, although these declines are neither simple nor dramatic. For example, verbal IQ and short-term memory remain fairly stable, but performance IQ and long-term memory become less effective.

5. That dementia is a gradual deterioration of intellectual abilities over several years until functioning becomes impaired.

6. That some cases of dementia are caused by factors such as medication or depression and are reversable but most cases are irreversible and due to such factors as Alzheimer's disease (in which neuronal degeneration occurs) or vascular diseases.

7. That there is no known treatment for dementia. Most dementia patients are in the care of their families and support for these families is valuable, specially when they must decide about institutionalization.

8. That delirium is a clouded state of consciousness characterized by difficulty in concentrating and maintaining a directed stream of though.

9. That there is a tendency to attribute the behavior of the aged to the fact that they are older. This can lead to erroneous conclusions about the effects of aging and cause us to overlook the individual's uniqueness.

10. Despite assumptions to the contrary, psychological problems such as depression, paranoid disorder, substance abuse, and hypochondria may actually be less prevalent among the aged than among younger groups.

11. That individual over 65 are three times as likely to commit suicide as are younger adults.

12. That most older adults maintain sexual interest and engage in sexual activity although there may be a general slowing of the sexual response cycle and the intensity of sexual arousal may not be as great.

13. That older adults do not seem to be getting their share of mental health services.

14. Regardless of whether they are cared for in the community or in a nursing home, giving the aged responsibility for self-care, planning, and control over their lives is important to their continued psychological and physical well-being.

KEY TERMS

Age effects (p. 433)

Cohort effects (p. 433)

Time of measurement effects (p. 433)

Dementia (p. 4340

Delirium (p. 446)

STUDY QUESTIONS

CONCEPTS & METHODS IN THE STUDY OF OLDER ADULTS (p. 433 - 434)

1. Identify four basic concepts in studying older adults (including three measurement effects that make data difficult to interpret). (p. 433 - 434)

SOME BASIC FACTS ABOUT OLDER ADULTS (p. 434 - 440)

2. Summarize eleven basic facts about older adults (p. 434 - 440)

BRAIN DISORDERS OF OLD AGE (p. 440 - 450)

3. Distinguish between two forms of brain disorder that often affect the elderly. For each form describe common causes, diagnostic procedures, and treatment. (p. 440 - 450)

PSYCHOLOGICAL DISORDERS OF OLD AGE (p. 450 - 461)

4. Why has little attention been paid to psychological problems in the elderly? (p. 450)

5. The text describes depression and paranoia in depth. For each identify, how common it is, how it differs in older people, possible causes, and treatment. (p. 450 - 455)

6. Briefly discuss the issues regarding schizophrenia and substance abuse in the elderly. (p. 455 - 457)

7. Describe the causes and treatment of three other psychological problems among the elderly. (p. 457 - 459)

8. How does sexual activity change with age? Briefly describe the social and physiological bases for these changes. (p. 459 - 461)

GENERAL ISSUES IN TREATMENT AND CARE (p. 461 - 469)

9. Identify two reasons the elderly do not receive their just share of mental health services. (p. 461 - 462)

10. What are the disadvantages of nursing homes for the elderly and why? What needs to be done in order to provide effective community-based alternatives (p. 462 - 466)

11. Summarize the major content and process issues in providing therapy to older adults. (p. 466 - 467)

SELF-TEST, CHAPTER 17

MULTIPLE-CHOICE

1. Which of the following statements about older adults is true?
    A. Men live longer than women on the average
    B. The number of very old people is expected to increase
    C. Serious declines in verbal intelligence begin about age 60
    D. Research shows that older people have more rigid, inflexible personalities

2. The term "dementia" refers to
    A. Confusion resulting from physiological imbalances
    B. Psychotic behavior in elderly people whatever it's cause
    C. Reversible brain disorders
    D. Any gradual intellectual deterioration

3. Dementia of the Alzheimer type is caused by
    A. Degeneration of cortical brain cells
    B. Hardening of the arteries
    C. Lack of social stimulation
    D. Nutritional deficiencies

4. Depression among older individuals
    A. Is less common than many other psychological problems
    B. Is primarily the result of normal aging processes
    C. Can often be treated through psychotherapy
    D. Often results from retirement

5. Hearing losses and social isolation contribute importantly to ____________ among the elderly
    A. Depression
    B. Paranoia
    C. Schizophrenia
    D. Hypocondriasis

6. Which of the following rarely appears for the first time in elderly individuals?
   A. Depression
   B. Paranoia
   C. Schizophrenia
   D. Hypocondriasis

7. Hypocondriasis may develop among older individuals because they
   A. Find it difficult to express concerns in psychological terms
   B. Have more physical problems as they become older
   C. Are encouraged to over-report problems by social welfare programs
   D. Have more free time to ruminate on their troubles

8. Suicide among older individuals is
   A. Rare compared to younger individuals
   B. Usually a plea for help and attention
   C. More common among women
   D. Typically successful

9. Which of the following best describes physiological changes in sexual responsiveness of older individuals
   A. Responsiveness is unchanged in physically healthy individuals
   B. Responsiveness slows but is still possible
   C. Responsiveness and interest declines rapidly
   D. Changes in responsiveness are primarily due to social factors

10. The primary problem with nursing home care provided the elderly according to the text is
   A. Lack of access to adequate facilities
   B. Brutality and neglect by nursing home staff
   C. Excessive care that discourages independence
   D. Families who use nursing homes as a dumping ground

11. Therapy with the elderly should NOT focus on
    A. Making plans for possible death
    B. Examining philosophical and religious values
    C. Coping with realistic life concerns
    D. Providing the best possible custodial care

SHORT ANSWER

1. The apparent financial conservativism of old people today may actually be due to the fact that they grew up during the great depression. This would be called a ____________.

2. How serious a problem are physical illnesses for most older people?

3. How significant are learning and memory loses for most older people?

4. How may societal expectations about old age effect older individuals?

5. It is best to be conservative in diagnosing senile dementia because . . .

6. List several common causes of delirium in older people.

7. Most psychological disorders in older people result from . . .

8. What appears to be the most effective treatment for insomnia and sleeplessness among the elderly?

9. What happens to sexual interests and activity as people get older?

10. Community-based services for the elderly should attempt to . . .

ANSWERS TO SELF-TEST, CHAPTER 17

MULTIPLE-CHOICE

1. A (p. 434)
2. D (p. 441)
3. A (p. 441-442)
4. C (p. 452)
5. B (p. 453)
6. C (p. 455)
7. A (p. 457)
8. D (p. 459)
9. B (p. 460)
10. C (p. 462-463)
11. D (p. 462)

SHORT ANSWER

1. Cohort effect. (p. 433)

2. Older people do decline physically and chronic illnesses are common but most are not severely limited by physical illnesses at least until after 75. (p. 436-437)

3. Research shows some slowing but this may be of little practical significance. (p. 437-438)

4. Older people may be treated as more limited than they are thus indirectly encouraging their decline. (p. 440)

5. Many temporary and reversible (treatable) conditions produce similar symptoms. (p. 443)

6. Intoxication from prescription drugs, metabolic & nutritional imbalances, illness, stress. (p. 447)

7. Realities of being elderly - or pre-existing problems. Not age or physical decline as such. (p. 450-451)

8. Reassurance that they need less sleep. Training in relaxation and good sleep habits. (p. 458)

9. They continue to have sexual interest and capacity. Some physical slowing but interest may remain. (p. 459-461)

10. Provide a range of services which can be matched to individual needs in order to encourage the elderly to live as independently as possible. (p. 465)

18 Insight Therapy

OVERVIEW

The previous chapter completed the text's discussion of major forms of abnormal behavior. Chapter 18 begins the last section of the text which describes major forms of treatment and related issues.

The first two chapters in the section discuss types of insight therapy and behavior therapy. These are the two major approaches to treatment in contemporary psychology. Chapter 20 will discuss other major approaches to treating psychological problems. Chapter 21 deals with legal and ethical issues in treatment.

CHAPTER SUMMARY

Insight therapies (Chapter 18) most closely fit the general understanding of "psychotherapy". Research into psychotherapy is complicated by The Placebo Effect, the tendency of patients to improve due to general factors rather than specific techniques.

Insight therapies assume that behavior changes as clients develop increased awareness of themselves and the conscious or unconscious motivations behind their behavior. Two major schools have emerged. Psychoanalytic Therapy, following Freud, sees problems as arising because individuals have never resolved childhood conflicts between their inner desires and external social reality demands. Psychoanalysis tries to uncover these repressed conflicts so they may be re-examined from an adult perspective.

Humanistic and Existential Therapies focus more on potentials for psychological growth and on factors that may inhibit and distort that growth. Humanists such as Rogers stress nonjudgmental acceptance by the therapist enables clients to understand themselves more accurately and to trust their inner desires for growth. Existentialists agree that all individuals have an inner drive to grow while emphasizing each person's ability to make choices. Both schools emphasize the need for therapists to understand and accept the client's perspective.

Perls' gestalt therapy is a variation on humanistic therapy which emphasizes living in the present and uses many techniques to help clients become aware of and accept their present feelings.

There is little research to show that improvement during insight therapy occurs for the reasons emphasized by the various theories. Some theorists deny that therapy can be understood and studied using scientific research methods.

STUDY OBJECTIVES

After studying Chapter 18 you should know:

1. That psychotherapy is an interpersonal influence process that is not readily distinguished from other helping relationships (such as friendships). Professionals typically work with people who have not been helped elsewhere.

2. The placebo effect, a part of all therapies, refers to an improvement that is attributable to expectations of help, rather than to a specific active ingredient.

3. That insight is the major goal of psychoanalytic, humanistic, existential, and gestalt therapies.

4. That in traditional psychoanalysis, free associations, resistance, dream analysis, interpretation, and transference are the major therapeutic tools used to achieve insight.

5. That ego analysts share many of Freud's views but place greater emphasis on the conscious mind and are more likely to deal with current problems by being directive as well as analyzing the past.

6. That research generally does not provide strong support regarding the effectiveness of analytic therapy when compared to improvement over time, although many of the concepts in analytic therapy make it particularly difficult to evaluate.

7. That psychotherapy outcome research evaluates the effectiveness of a treatment in comparison to an alternative such as no treatment while psychotherapy process research links therapeutic interactions with therapy outcome.

8. That the concept of free will is emphasized by humanistic, existential, and Gestalt therapist.

9. That Carl Rogers argued that therapy should be directed by the client, and that the therapist's major goal is to help the client by being warm, genuine, and empathetic.

10. That existential therapists emphasize authenticity, awareness, and the exercise of free choice - which carries with it the confrontation of some painful realities. Thus they are less optimistic about the innate qualities of humans than are humanistic therapists.

11. Fritz Perls's therapy highlights the here and now and makes use of a variety of techniques in order to help people become aware of their present desires.

KEY TERMS

Insight (vs. action) therapy (p. 474)

Placebo effect (p. 474)

Psychoanalysis (p. 475)

Free association (p. 475)

Resistance (p. 476)

Transference neurosis (p. 477)

Countertransference (p. 478)

Ego analysis (p. 479)

Harry Stack Sullivan (p. 481)

Parataxic distortion (p. 481)

Outcome research (p. 483)

Process research (p. 485)

Client-centered therapy (p. 485)

Unconditional positive regard (p. 486)

Empathy (p. 486)

Existential therapy (p. 489)

Gestalt therapy (p. 491)

STUDY QUESTIONS

THE PLACEBO EFFECT (p 474 - 475)

1. Why is "psychotherapy" difficult to define? What role may the placebo effect play in psychotherapy? (p. 466 - 475)

PSYCHOANALYTIC THERAPY (p. 475 - 485)

2. What is the basic assumption of psychoanalysis? Describe six basic techniques of psychoanalysis and explain how each contributes to treatment. (p. 475 - 479)

3. How do ego analysts differ from classical analysis in their views on (1) the role of the ego and (2) the source of energy or gratification for the ego? (p. 479 - 481)

4. Describe two ways in which Harry Stack Sullivan differed from Freud. (p. 481)

5. Why has it been difficult to evaluate analytic therapy--or other forms of psychotherapy? Briefly summarize the results of outcome and process research. (p. 481 - 485)

HUMANISTIC & EXISTENTIAL THERAPIES (p. 485 - 496)

6. Summarize Carl Roger's client-centered views on human nature and personality development. (p. 485 - 486)

7. What is the role of a Rogerian therapist? Describe three qualities of a therapist in this role explaining the importance of the third quality. (p. 486 - 488)

8. What kind of research has Rogers done to evaluate his theory and with what results? Identify six criticisms of his theory. (p. 488 - 489)

9. According to existential philosophy, what are the consequences of self-awareness and of becoming. Summarize four goals of existential therapy (p. 489 - 490)

10. Why do existentialists reject scientific evaluation of their approach? (p. 491 - 492)

11. Summarize the basic concepts of Gestalt therapy in terms of (1) the influence of individual needs, (2) the individual as actor, and (3) the here and now. Give some examples of Gestalt techniques. (p. 491 - 495)

12. Summarize the text's evaluation of Gestalt therapy in five points. (Look for: overall evaluation, theoretical parsimony, strengths and weaknesses of Gestalt "responsibility", view of human goodness, and Perls as an individual.) (p. 495 - 496)

SELF-TEST, CHAPTER 18

MULTIPLE-CHOICE

1. The placebo effect in psychotherapy is best defined as the effect of
   A. Free association
   B. Medication
   C. Expectancy
   D. Phenomenology

2. Resistance is said to occur in psychoanalysis when the patient
   A. Treats the therapist like a parent figure
   B. Avoids free associating
   C. Refuses to accept an interpretation
   D. Rambles on about whatever is on his/her mind

3. Transference is important in psychoanalysis because it
   A. Helps patients see the childhood origins of their problems
   B. Gives patients a sense of positive regard
   C. Enables patients to free associate
   D. Can block a cure if it is expressed

4. Harry Stack Sullivan emphasized that disturbed interpersonal relations in childhood produce
   A. Ego analyses
   B. Oedipal conflicts
   C. Countertransferences
   D. Parataxic distortions

5. Evaluating the effectiveness of psychoanalysis is difficult because of disagreements over
   A. Criteria for improvement
   B. The definition of free association
   C. What techniques Freud actually used
   D. What kinds of problems it should be effective with

6. Humanistic and existential therapists hold that free will
   A. Is only a phenomenological illusion
   B. Is an important characteristic of all people
   C. Can exist if childhood conflicts are resolved
   D. Must be controlled if growth is to occur

7. In order to be effective a therapist must, according to Roger's client-centered theory
   A. Avoid getting caught up in countertransferences
   B. Actively encourage the client to adopt improved ways of living
   C. Remain objective and detached from the client's conflicts
   D. Understand the world from the client's point of view

8. In existential therapy the concept of "Becoming" means that
   A. Present problems reflect past conflicts
   B. Behavior change follows insight and increased awareness
   C. People are constantly evolving
   D. People have the capacity for self-awareness

9. Which of the following therapies focuses on helping people become more aware of their here-and-now experiences and desires
   A. Psychoanalysis
   B. Client centered
   C. Existential
   D. Gestalt

10. In evaluating Gestalt therapy the text points out that it
   A. Discourages social commitment and responsibility
   B. Does not have a clear philosophical or theoretical basis
   C. Systematically discourages research on therapy techniques
   D. Overemphasizes the role of childhood conflicts

SHORT ANSWER

1. What is the basic assumption of insight psychotherapy?

2. Why do psychoanalysts attempt to remain detached from their patients?

3. Briefly describe how ego analysts view people (as compared to traditional psychoanalysis).

4. What kinds of people and problems are most likely to benefit from psychoanalysis?

5. Summarize current views on the effectiveness of psychoanalysis.

6. Summarize Carl Roger's view of personality development and growth.

7. The text criticizes Rogerian-based therapy research for not paying enough attention to . . .

8. Why do existential therapists avoid doing research on the effectiveness of their techniques?

9. What is the general purpose of gestalt therapy techniques?

10. What do Gestalt therapists such as Perls urge clients to be responsible for?

ANSWERS TO SELF-TEST, CHAPTER 18

MULTIPLE-CHOICE

1. C (p. 474-475)
2. B (p. 476)
3. A (p. 477-478)
4. D (p. 481)
5. A (p. 482)
6. B (p. 485)
7. D (p. 485)
8. C (p. 489-490)
9. D (p. 491-492)
10. A (p. 495)

SHORT ANSWER

1. That people can control and change behavior if they develop understanding of what causes or motivates it. (p. 474)

2. They feel that offering suggestions and comfort would provide short-term help at best and would delay development of transference and long-term improvement. (p. 478-479)

3. View people as able to control their environment and instinctual drives enabling them to postpone and control urges. (p. 480-481)

4. Educated verbal people with neurotic, not psychotic, problems. (p. 483)

5. It's effectiveness is difficult to measure. It is not clearly more effective than other methods, placebos, or simply passage of time. (p. 483-484)

6. People innately seek to grow, to actualize or develop their potentials, and will seek ways to do so. (p. 485-486)

7. How people's actual behavior changes following therapy. (p. 488)

8. Their therapy is based on philosophical, not scientific, views. They consider science dehumanizing. (p. 490-491)

9. Help clients get in touch with here-and-now feelings. (p. 492-494)

10. Taking care of themselves by recognizing and accepting responsibility for meeting their own needs. (p. 492,495)

19 Behavior Therapy

OVERVIEW

Chapter 19 is the second of three chapters on therapies for psychological problems. Chapters 18 and 19 discuss the two major approaches to therapy in contemporary psychology: insight and behavior therapies. Insight approaches grew primarily out of the experiences of therapists talking with disturbed individuals. In contrast, behavior therapies grew out of scientific research traditions within psychology. Insight therapies seek to develop increased self-insight and awareness on the assumption that behavior will change naturally as individuals understand the bases for their disordered actions. Behavior therapies use scientific principles to study disordered behavior and to develop methods for changing it.

After Chapter 19 the text will discuss some other popular therapy techniques such as group, family, community, and somatic therapy. The last chapter will cover legal and ethical issues in abnormal psychology.

CHAPTER SUMMARY

The chapter summarizes a variety of behavior therapies which have developed out of research models of behavior. <u>Counterconditioning</u> seeks to change classically conditioned responses to stimuli. For example, systematic desensitization seeks to eliminate unrealistic fear responses by gradually introducing the stimulus under anxiety inhibiting conditions. Aversion therapy attempts to sensitize negative responses to inappropriately attractive stimuli.

Operant Conditioning uses rewards and punishment to modify behaviors. For example, token economies systematically reward appropriate behaviors among hospitalized patients. Operant principles are also used to help insure that changes generalize after treatment is discontinued. Modeling and imitation are used to teach a wide variety of complex responses to situations.

As behavior therapy has matured, behavior therapists have become more flexible and have developed Cognitive Restructuring procedures to identify and change beliefs that may lead to inappropriate behaviors. Other behaviorists have developed Behavioral Medicine which applies scientific principles to the psychological aspects of traditionally medical problems.

Some Basic Issues in Behavioral Therapy remain although, with the newer methods, some of the old distinctions between insight and behavioral therapies are becoming increasingly blurred.

STUDY OBJECTIVES

After studying Chapter 19 you should know:

1. That behavior therapy involves the application of procedures developed by experimental psychologists. It is characterized more by its search for rigorous standards of proof than by an allegiance to a particular set of concepts.

2. That, in conterconditioning, a response to a given stimulus is eliminated by eliciting different behavior in the presence of the stimulus.

3. That systematic desensitization is a fear reduction technique that involves pairing, through imagination, increasingly feared events with a simultaneous state of deep muscle relaxation.

4. That aversion therapy involves pairing an aversive stimulus with an unwanted thought, emotion, or behavior in order to reduce it. There are questions about the ethics and efficacy of aversion therapy.

5. That operant conditioning therapy techniques involve the delineation of rules of expected behavior and the systematic reinforcement of behavior which meets these rules. It seems to work best with clients with limited cognitive capabilities and in situations where the therapist can exercise considerable environmental control.

6. That obtaining the generalization of treatment effects across time and settings is a goal that can be difficult to achieve without the use of techniques designed to promote it.

7. That modeling techniques have been used to help treat a wide variety of problems. However modeling involves more than simple imitation and would appear to rely upon a complex set of cognitive processes.

8. That behavior therapies have more recently been concerned with altering cognitive processes, with rational-emotive therapy, Beck's cognitive therapy, and social problem solving as examples of cognitive restructuring techniques.

9. That cognitive behavior therapists in some ways are returning to the early roots of experimental psychology which focused on mental processes while retaining the emphasis on behavior change as a therapeutic goal.

10. That the cognitive behavior therapist's interest in the way the client perceives the world brings behavior therapy closer to the views of the humanist and the existentialist.

11. That behavioral medicine involves the integration of behavioral and medical science so as to aid in the prevention, diagnosis, treatment and rehabilitation of medical diseases.

12. That behavior therapy, in practice, in more complex than it may appear from the description of techniques. Behavior therapists seek to treat underlying factors, emphasize therapeutic relationships, and combine techniques in broad-spectrum treatments.

13. That there are some who see the hope of rapprochement between behavior therapy and psychoanalysis as analysts become more active and behaviorists more sensitive to childhood and subtle factors.

KEY TERMS

Behavior therapy (p. 498)

Counter-conditioning (p. 498)

Systematic desensitization (p. 498)

Aversion therapy (p. 501)

Token economy (p. 503)

Self-reinforcement (p. 507)

Modeling (p. 508)

Cognitive restructuring (p. 511)

Rational-emotional therapy (p. 511)

Social problem solving (p. 516)

Behavioral medicine (p. 517)

Biofeedback (p. 521)

STUDY QUESTIONS

1. What is "behavior therapy"? What does it assume? (p. 498)

COUNTERCONDITIONING (p. 498 - 503)

2. What is the basic principle of counterconditioning? Briefly describe two counterconditioning methods and their effectiveness. (p. 498 - 503)

OPERANT CONDITIONING (p. 503 - 508)

3. Describe the basic idea of operant conditioning therapies. Describe two areas in which operant conditioning procedures have been applied. (p. 503 - 505)

4. What forms of therapy need to be concerned about generalization of treatment results? Describe five methods used by behavior therapists to increase generalization. (p. 505 - 508)

MODELING (p. 508 - 510)

5. Briefly describe the use of modeling to treat various problems. How did modeling influence interest in the role of cognition? (p. 508 - 510)

COGNITIVE RESTRUCTURING (p. 510 - 517)

6. Describe how Ellis and Beck apply cognitive restructuring noting their emphasis on behavioral as well as cognitive changes. Explain the basic difference between these two approaches. (p. 510 - 516)

7. Describe the cognitive therapy of social problem solving. Summarize four general reflections or comments concerning cognitive behavior therapy made in the text. (p. 516 - 517)

BEHAVIORAL MEDICINE (p. 517 - 522)

8. How is behavioral medicine best defined? Describe three areas of interest in behavioral medicine. (p. 517 - 522)

SOME BASIC ISSUES IN BEHAVIOR THERAPY (p. 522 - 526)

9. Summarize six basic issues underlying contemporary behavior therapy. (p. 522 - 524)

10. What synthesis of psychoanalysis and behavior therapy does Wachtel suggest? Identify five possible benefits of this rapprochement. (p. 524 - 526)

SELF-TEST, CHAPTER 19

MULTIPLE-CHOICE

1. Behavior therapy is based on the assumption that
   A. All behavior is learned through reinforcement
   B. Scientific methods can produce effective clinical procedures
   C. Insight is not a necessary prerequisite for behavior to change
   D. Therapy should be limited to procedures that are proven effective by research

2. Research indicates that the effectiveness of systematic desensitization
   A. Depends on cognitive restructuring of the underlying conflict
   B. Does not persist over time
   C. Is superior to insight therapy
   D. Can be attributed to placebo effects

3. What is the name for the behavioral procedures used in hospital wards which give patients extra privileges in exchange for ward work and self-care behaviors?
   A. Systematic desensitization
   B. Token economies
   C. Modeling
   D. Behavioral medicine

4. Behavioral therapists have found that self-reinforcement
   A. Can help treatment gains generalize to other situations
   B. Must be used as part of cognitive restructuring methods
   C. Is an important procedure for overcoming unrealistic fears
   D. Is not an effective procedure in most situations

5. Which of the following has been used to explain why behavior therapy patients may find excuses not to follow treatment procedures which they have agreed to

   A. Social problem solving
   B. Systematic desensitization
   C. Counter conditioning
   D. Secondary gain

6. Modeling procedures were important because they showed behavior therapists the importance of

   A. Sticking to observable behaviors
   B. Classical conditioning
   C. Operant conditioning
   D. Cognitive processes

7. Ellis' rational-emotive therapy is based on the thesis that emotional problems are caused by

   A. Classical conditioning
   B. Understandable responses to emotionally traumatic events
   C. Irrational things people say to themselves
   D. Unspoken cognitive conflicts

8. ____________ seeks to give patients experiences which lead them to discover that their thoughts are illogical

   A. Implosion
   B. Self-control
   C. Beck's Cognitive therapy
   D. Social problem solving

9. Which of the following is <u>not</u> a step in social problem solving procedures

   A. Identifying what the problem may be
   B. Determining if a solution is needed
   C. Evaluating consequences of possible solutions
   D. Implement a decision & evaluate it's effectiveness

10. Behavioral medicine procedures are being developed

   A. As an alternative to medical treatment
   B. To encourage people to seek medical treatment
   C. Despite the lack of proof of their effectiveness
   D. To treat psychological aspects of medical conditions

SHORT ANSWER

1. Describe the method of systematic desensitization.

2. Briefly summarize two reasons that aversion therapy is controversial.

3. How does intermittent reinforcement encourage generalization of treatment results?

4. Briefly describe four other methods used to promote generalization of treatment changes.

5. Explain how modeling is used in behavioral therapy.

6. How does Ellis go about helping people change their irrational self-statements in rational-emotive therapy?

7. How does Beck's therapeutic approach differ from that of Ellis?

8. In what way is behavioral therapy becoming similar to humanistic & existential therapy?

9. What is "behavioral medicine".

10. Do behavioral therapists deal with symptoms or with the true causes of behavior? Explain.

ANSWERS TO SELF-TEST, CHAPTER 19

MULTIPLE-CHOICE

1. B (p. 498)
2. C (p. 500)
3. B (p. 503)
4. A (p. 507)
5. D (p. 507)
6. D (p. 510)
7. C (p. 511)
8. C (p. 514-516)
9. B (p. 516)
10. D (p. 517-520)

SHORT ANSWER

1. Client is deeply relaxed, then is asked to imagine series of increasingly anxiety-provoking situations. (p. 499)

2. A) Ethics of inflicting pain even when clients agree, B) Effectiveness doubtful unless combined with other methods. (p. 501-503)

3. Helps behavior endure so natural reinforcers (praise, etc.) can become effective. (p. 505)

4. 1) Modifying environment to support changed behavior, 2) Encouraging clients to recognize and reinforce themselves for good behavior, 3) Eliminating "secondary gain", 4) Encouraging clients to attribute results to their own efforts. (p. 506-507

5. The model demonstrates desirable or effective behavior which the client can imitate. (p. 508-509)

6. By using rational explanation and persuasive logic. Helps client realize their self-talk is irrational and leads to problems. (p. 511-512)

7. Beck collaborates with client as they seek to discover ineffective assumptions together. (Ellis identifies irrationality and explains it to client) (p. 515-516)

8. Behavior therapy is coming to emphasize cognitive methods which share, with humanism, the view that our perceptions and understandings of the world are the cause of behavior. (p. 517)

9. Combines behavioral & medical fields to develop psychological procedures for improving physical health and treating physical problems. (p. 517-520)

10. Behaviorists do not, like psychoanalysts, assume true causes must involve unconscious or childhood factors. They seek the most important causes of behavior which may be in the current situation. (p. 522)

20 Group and Marital Therapy, Community Psychology, and Somatic Treatment

OVERVIEW

This is the last of three chapters exploring various treatment approaches. The previous two chapters presented insight and behavior therapies as two primary approaches to treatment. Despite marked differences in both goals and methods, these two approaches were seen as moving to a rapproachment at the end of Chapter 19. Chapter 20 discusses three other forms or approaches to treatment: group and marital, community, and somatic treatments.

The final chapter of the text will cover legal and ethical issues in abnormal psychology. Psychologists are often faced with dilemmas as they try to protect the rights of both their clients and of larger society. Legal issues will include criminal commitment (legal insanity, and competency to stand trial) and civil commitment for individuals judged dangerous to themselves or others. Ethical issues involve efforts to define and protect the rights of individuals as both therapy clients and research participants.

CHAPTER SUMMARY

Chapter 20 discusses; Group and marital treatment, Community treatment, and Somatic treatments. All three offer their own unique strengths. <u>Group and Marital Therapy</u> is most obviously related to the insight and behavior therapies. Therapy groups are not only economical, but they also offer opportunities to share with and learn from others and to get behind social facades. Family therapy looks at the special problems of family groups by considering the problems of the "identified patient" to be a manifestation of disturbances within the family itself. Research on these forms of treatment shows much promise.

<u>Community Psychology</u> seeks to prevent problems from developing by promoting changes in groups, communities, and society at large. Often community psychology is carried out in community mental health centers which work within the community to prevent or alleviate problems, thus minimizing the need for hospitalization. Prevention of problems has remained, however, an elusive goal.

<u>Somatic Treatment</u> uses physical means to treat behavior. Psychoactive drugs have proven useful in treating a wide variety of problems. Drugs do, however, have side effects which can be serious. Usually they need to be used in conjunction with other therapies to treat all aspects of an individual's problem. Drugs have virtually eliminated the need for more radical earlier treatments such as psychosurgery although electroconvulsive shock treatment remains apparently effective for profound depression.

STUDY OBJECTIVES

After studying Chapter 20 you should know:

1. That group therapy is more economical but most therapists suggest that there are additional unique benefits to group therapy, such as vicarious learning, group pressure to change, and the support in knowing that a problem is experienced by others.

2. That Jacob Moreno's psychodrama was probably the first from of group therapy.

3. That T-groups and sensitivity training groups are commonly used as growth experiences for well-functioning individuals. Learning to become more honest and open with others and obtaining feedback on interpersonal relationships are among the primary goals of these groups.

4. That some behavior therapy groups involve administering a treatment in much the same way that it would be offered in individual therapy, but other behavior therapy groups use the format to train skills that only can be learned in a group setting.

5. That research on group therapy, especially process research, is exceedingly difficult to conduct.

6. That marital and family therapists attribute many psychological difficulties to problems in family relationships. Therapists with this orientation see family members conjointly and often emphasize the importance of dealing with interpersonal conflicts and improving communication.

7. That community psychologists focus on the prevention of emotional disturbance using primary, secondary, and tertiary prevention.

8. That given their focus on prevention, community psychologists are likely to operate in the seeking mode rather than the waiting mode and are likely to target their interventions at the organizational or institutional levels rather than at the individual or small group levels.

9. That community mental health centers, suicide prevention centers, the use of the media to try to change life styles, halfway houses, and environmental psychology are all examples of community psychology efforts.

10. That in many ways community psychology has not lived up to its promise. Perhaps its' assumptions that mental disorders have environmental causes and that community psychology interventions are targeted at the correct environmental conditions are not correct.

11. That the major drug therapies include: the minor tranquilizers to treat anxiety and psychosomatic disorders; the neuroleptics of hyperactivity;

antidepressants; and lithium carbonate to treat bipolar disorder.

12. That the commonly used drug therapies have been found to be superior to placebo effects. However, in many cases, psychotherapy may add to the effects of medication and, in some cases, may be equal or superior to drug therapy.

KEY TERMS

Psychodrama (p. 528)

Sensitivity training (p. 529)

Marathons (p. 531)

Prevention (primary, secondary, tertiary) (p. 541)

Waiting mode & seeking mode (p. 541)

Tranquilizers (p. 554)

Neuroleptics (p. 555)

Stimulants (p. 557)

Antidepressants (p. 557)

Lithium carbonate (p. 558)

ECT (p. 560)

STUDY QUESTIONS

GROUP AND MARITAL THERAPY (p. 528 - 541)

1. Describe the rationale behind psychodrama. (p. 528 - 529)

2. How are the goals of sensitivity training or encounter groups different from the goals of other psychotherapies? How do levels of communication and leader roles facilitate these goals? (p. 529 - 531)

3. Summarize several examples of behavior therapy groups. (Note that some of these examples use a group approach primarily to economize.) (p. 532 - 533)

4. Evaluate group therapy in terms of testimonials, transfer of skills, and research. Review the conclusions of research, especially in terms of changes in self-concept and behavior of group participants? (p. 533 -534)

5. Summarize the views of marital therapists on; the inevitability of marital conflict (p. 534), developing positive feelings (p. 538), and developing communication (p. 539). Give some examples of how other therapy approaches are applied to families. (p. 536)

6. How might marital therapy concepts be applied to nonmarital problems and divorce? Summarize research into marital and family therapy. (p. 540 - 541)

COMMUNITY PSYCHOLOGY (p. 541 - 554)

7. Summarize the views of community psychology on the topics of prevention, delivery mode, and the influence of social values on how community oriented therapists operate. (p. 541 - 544)

8. Describe community mental health centers in terms of their objectives, use of paraprofessionals, and emphasis on education. Describe and evaluate four examples of community-oriented efforts. (p. 544 - 552)

9. Evaluate the effectiveness of community psychology in four areas. How well have mental health centers fulfilled their original hopes and why (or why not)? (p. 552 - 554)

SOMATIC TREATMENT (p. 554 - 561)

10. The text lists five groups of drugs in common use. For each group, summarize (1) common examples, (2) common uses, and (3) effectiveness as shown by research. (p. 554 - 559)

11. Summarize the original and present uses for psychosurgery and convulsive therapy. (p. 559 - 561)

SELF-TEST, CHAPTER 20

MULTIPLE-CHOICE

1. ____________ is a form of therapy designed to promote personal growth in individuals who are not seriously disturbed.
   A. Psychodrama
   B. Sensitivity training
   C. Conjoint therapy
   D. Aftercare

2. The role of a T-group leader includes
   A. Being a fully participating member of the group
   B. Providing insights for group members
   C. Helping members develop accurate judgments of each other
   D. Guiding the group into desirable directions

3. Evaluations of group therapy have failed to answer the question of whether
   A. Members feel better about themselves after therapy
   B. Many members are harmed by their experiences in therapy
   C. Changes made in therapy transfer to the real world
   D. All of the above

4. Marital therapists generally agree that conflicts in marital relationships are
   A. Due to the unique characteristics of marriage itself
   B. Reduced once the couple have children
   C. The result of conflicts which the individuals had before they married
   D. Inevitable in any long-term emotional relationship

5. A common goal in almost all marital therapy is to
   A. Improve sexual functioning
   B. Improve communication within the family
   C. Reduce quarrels between marital partners
   D. Minimize the destructive impact of disturbed family members on the rest of the family

6. Which of the following is an example of primary prevention in community psychology?
   A. Educating the public on diet and exercise
   B. Developing aftercare programs for ex-mental patients
   C. Court-ordered counseling for young delinquents
   D. Suicide prevention centers

7. According to the text, suicide prevention centers.
   A. Are relatively ineffective as suicidal individuals are unlikely to call them
   B. Are much more effective if staffed by professionals rather than volunteers
   C. Are more helpful than friends in preventing suicide
   D. Should be continued despite lack of evidence of their effectiveness

8. A general problem with most drugs used for treating psychological disorders is that
   A. They have a high potential to become addictive
   B. Their effectiveness is unknown
   C. They have side-effects which may be serious
   D. They gradually lose effectiveness for many patients

9. The use of psychosurgery has declined in recent decades because
   A. The procedures were very expensive
   B. The procedures produced serious side-effects
   C. The procedures did not significantly alter behavior
   D. Lack of research into improved procedures

10. Electroconvulsive shock therapy (ECT)
   A. Is effective in treating profound depression
   B. Is rarely used because of serious physical and psychological side-effects
   C. Is prohibited by law in most states
   D. Is commonly used in treating schizophrenia

SHORT ANSWER

1. Give two advantages of group & marital therapy over individual therapy.

2. In ____________ groups individuals learn and practice more effective ways of relating to other people.

3. What is meant by saying that community psychology operates in the seeking mode?

4. What is the goal of community psychologists working at the organizational & institutional levels?

5. describe the different services offered by community mental health centers (in five areas).

6. Describe a study that used community psychology methods to change harmful life styles.

7. What benefits can halfway houses and aftercare facilities provide according to research?

8. What are the advantages of using paraprofessionals in community mental health?

9. What are the advantages & disadvantages of phenothiazine drugs in treating schizophrenia.

10. What are the advantages and disadvantages of stimulant drugs in the treatment of hyperactivity?

ANSWERS TO SELF-TEST, CHAPTER 20

MULTIPLE-CHOICE

1. B (p. 529) 2. A (p. 531) 3. C (p. 533)
4. D (p. 534-535) 5. B (p. 539) 6. A (p. 541)
7. D (p. 547) 8. C (p. 554-559) 9. B (p. 560)
10. A (p. 561)

SHORT ANSWER

1. 1) More economical, 2) Individual can receive encouragement & feedback from others. (p. 528)

2. Social-skills training (p. 532)

3. It reaches out to offer help (rather than waiting for people to make appointments) and to improve social conditions. (p. 541)

4. To improve the mental health of society by changing society's organizations and institutions. (p. 542-543)

5. Outpatient therapy (affordable, in the community), Short-term inpatient care, Day treatment, 24 hour emergency services, Consultation & education. (p. 544)

6. Used mass media campaigns, educational groups, etc. to tell community how to reduce cardiovascular disease by changes in diet, smoking, exercise. (p. 548-549)

7. Enable patients to live and function in the community (stay out of mental hospitals) thus reducing overall health care costs. (p. 549-550)

8. Clients can more easily identify with, work with. learn from, paraprofessionals from the same community & background. (p. 552)

9. Effective in reducing bizarre behavior making it possible for schizophrenics to leave the hospital. Little effect on negative symptoms so that their functioning remains limited and readmissions common. They must continue to take the drugs which can have serious side effects. (p. 555-557)

10. Effectively reduce impulsivity and overactivity, improve attention, etc. But do not improve (& may hurt) school performance, have adverse short and long-term side effects. (p. 557)

21 Legal and Ethical Issues

OVERVIEW

The last three chapters dealt with various forms, techniques, or approaches to treatment. These included insight oriented therapies, behavioral therapies, and a variety of specialized approaches. This, the final chapter of the text, turns to legal and ethical issues in abnormal psychology.

CHAPTER SUMMARY

Psychologists struggle with many legal and ethical issues or dilemmas. Legal issues develop when an individual's mental condition becomes an issue in court. In Criminal Commitment cases, issues develop when individuals accused of crimes are found incompetent to stand trial or are acquitted by reason of insanity at the time of the crime. In Civil Commitment cases, individuals not accused of crimes may be committed to institutions if they are considered mentally ill and dangerous to themselves or others. It is not clear that either of these legal procedures are fair to the individuals involved or to larger society. Recent court rulings have clarified the legal rights of committed individuals, especially those civilly committed. These include rights to have legal counsel, protection from self-incrimination, etc. and rights to be treated in the least restrictive environment possible, to actually receive treatment, and to refuse treatment in some cases.

Ethical Issues in Therapy and Research cover a very broad area of individual rights. For example, psychologists recognize ethical obligations to obtain the informed consent of others before involving them in research and treatment. Yet research participants may behave differently if they completely understand what is being investigated and disturbed patients, under pressure from family and society, may not be able to choose freely or even to understand the consequences of their decisions. Therapists are also ethically and legally obligated to respect the confidentiality of their patients yet they may have to break confidentiality, for example, if their patients are endangering themselves or others. Such problems are very real ethical dilemmas that do not always have easy answers.

STUDY OBJECTIVES

After studying Chapter 21 you should know:

1. That criminal commitment is the process by which mentally ill individuals who have broken the law can be committed to a prison hospital.

2. That civil commitment is a set of procedures by which a person who has not broken the law can be incarcerated in a mental hospital.

3. That the insanity defense can be based on one of three historically important grounds: the McNaghten rule refers to the inability to distinguish right from wrong; the "irresistible impulse" concept suggests that a person is not guilty by reason of insanity if a pathological impulse or drive that could not be resisted was the cause of the crime; and the Durham test suggests that the insanity defense may be invoked if the unlawful act was a product of mental disease or defect.

4. That a mentally disturbed individual can be committed to a prison mental hospital if they are judged incompetent to understand the proceedings at the time of the trial.

5. That Thomas Szasz has argued that we should hold all individuals as being ascriptively responsible for their actions (i.e. no insanity defense) because the insanity defense is used as an excuse for overlooking pathological social conditions and blaming a "diseased mind" for acts that have political meaning.

6. That while the grounds for civil commitment vary from state to state, in virtually all states a person can be committed if they are (a) mentally ill and (b) unable to care for themselves or are a danger to self or others.

7. That there is debate as to how accurate mental health professionals are at predicting the future dangerousness of a mentally disturbed individual.

8. That there have been a number of recent legal developments which increase the protections for those people committed through criminal and civil proceedings. These include being cared for in the least restrictive alternate setting, having the right to treatment not just minimal custodial care, and having the right to refuse certain, particularly dangerous or noxious treatments.

9. That regulations have been formulated to protect the rights of subjects in psychological research, such as the concept of informed consent -- informing the subject of the risks involved in the research and of their right to freely accept or reject participation in the experiment

10. That the ethical codes of various mental health professions dictate that, with certain exceptions, the communication between patient and therapist must be kept confidential. Privileged communication laws extend this protection into the courts.

11. That therapists face additional ethical dilemmas in determining who is the client they are serving, what the goals for treatment should be, and what techniques should be used to achieve those goals.

KEY TERMS

Criminal commitment (p. 564)

Insanity (p. 568)

Incompetency to stand trial (p. 568)

Descriptive & Ascriptive responsibility (p. 569)

Civil commitment (p. 572)

Informed consent (p. 584)

Confidentiality (p. 587)

Privileged communication (p. 587)

STUDY QUESTIONS

CRIMINAL COMMITMENT (p. 564 - 572)

1. Summarize three landmark court decisions which yielded guidelines for defining legal insanity as well as the recent ALI guidelines. Why have these proven difficult in practice? (p. 564 - 566)

2. Read the case example (p. 566) and explain how it illustrates three additional problems with the concept of legal insanity. (p. 566 - 568)

3. Distinguish between "insanity" and "competency". What is the basic legal principle behind competency to stand trial? Compare competency to insanity in terms of (1) possible consequences and (2) clarity of guidelines. (p. 568 - 569)

4. Thomas Szasz presents an interesting but complex argument against criminal commitment. Explain his distinction between descriptive and ascriptive responsibility. What role does he fear insanity often plays in the courts? What alternative does he propose? (p. 569 - 570)

5. How does the text evaluate Szasz's position? What does the text suggest society do? (p. 570 - 572)

CIVIL COMMITMENT (p. 572 - 582)

6. Identify the common criteria and types of civil commitment. (p. 572 -574)

7. Identify two problems psychologists face in identifying "dangerous" individuals. Evaluate research on psychologists' ability to predict dangerousness. (574 - 575)

8. Summarize the recent trends in rates of involuntary commitment. Illustrate two reasons (one constitutional and one practical) that involuntary commitment remains an issue? (p. 575 - 576)

9. Summarize three recent trends protecting the rights of individuals who have been committed. How do Paul and Lentz propose to deal with these seemingly contradictory rights? (p. 576 - 582)

ETHICAL DILEMMAS IN THERAPY AND RESEARCH (p. 582 - 595)

10. Give two examples outside psychology that point to the need for ethical restraints in research. (p. 582 - 584)

11. Summarize six ethical dilemmas being sure to point out why each is a dilemma (i.e. why it is not easily resolved). (p. 584 - 595) Explain the distinction between confidentiality and privileged communication.

12. Summarize the textbook's concluding comments. (p. 595)

SELF-TEST, CHAPTER 21

MULTIPLE-CHOICE

1. The insanity defense
   A. Is frequently used in criminal trials
   B. Came into existence within the last 40 to 50 years
   C. Assumes that only disturbed individuals lack free will
   D. Is based on the mental state of the accused at the time of trial

2. Which of the following has NOT been used as a criterion of legal insanity
   A. Repeated criminal or antisocial conduct
   B. Not knowing right from wrong
   C. Irresistible impulse
   D. Mental disease or defect

3. __________ is based on the legal right of individuals to be present at their own trial and participate in their own defense.
   A. Insanity
   B. Competency
   C. Civil commitment
   D. Least restrictive environment

4. A police officer who kills someone in the line of duty would be described by Szasz as ____________ responsible
   A. Descriptively but not ascriptively
   B. Ascriptively but not descriptively
   C. Both descriptively and ascriptively
   D. Neither descriptively nor ascriptively

5. Mental health professionals are probably able to predict ____________ dangerousness of disturbed individuals.
   A. Both immediate and long-term
   B. Long-term but not immediate
   C. Immediate but not long-term
   D. Neither immediate nor long-term

6. At present there is considerable controversy concerning the rights of committed mental patients to
   A. Receive treatment
   B. Refuse treatment
   C. Legal counsel
   D. Confidentiality

7. Paul & Lentz propose to reconcile conflicts between rights to receive treatment, to refuse treatment, and to be treated in the least restrictive setting by requiring
   A. Treatment be limited to methods that are proven effective
   B. Consent of the individual or guardian to treatment
   C. Legal review when the patient does not agree with treatment decisions
   D. Patients to participate in methods that seek minimal goals

8. The distinction between confidentiality and privileged communication is that only privileged communication protects individuals from
   A. Being judged dangerous based on what they said
   B. Unethical practices of the therapist
   C. Having what they said revealed to others
   D. Having what they said revealed in court

9. ______________ refers to the ethical dilemma of psychologists faced with many individuals or interests who have simultaneous, conflicting, legitimate goals.
   A. Informed consent
   B. Who is the client
   C. Choice of goals
   D. Choice of techniques

10. The choice of goals in therapy is an ethical dilemma because
   A. Therapists cannot avoid subtly influencing the goals chosen by their patients
   B. Patients often seek goals which are inappropriate
   C. Patients may unwitingly sabotage therapy if they understand it's real goals
   D. Committed patients have a right to refuse treatment

SHORT ANSWER

1. Summarize the American Law Institute guidelines for defining criminal insanity.

2. What problems are faced by someone who succeeds in proving they are not guilty by reason of insanity (as shown by the illustration in the text)?

3. What is the difference between legal insanity and legal competency?

4. What is the rationale or basis for Szasz's case against the use of the insanity defense?

5. On what basis may individuals be committed to a mental hospital against their will (civil commitment)?

6. Identify three legal protections or rights being extended to mental patients by recent legal decisions.

7. Identify two sources of ethical restraints on contemporary research.

8. Define "informed consent".

9. Give several reasons (text had 5) why therapists may reveal things clients tell them even when state law provides privileged communication for therapy relationships.

10. Are there circumstances where therapists are justified in inflicting pain on patients?

ANSWERS TO SELF-TEST, CHAPTER 21

MULTIPLE-CHOICE

1. C (p. 565)
2. A (p. 565-566)
3. B (p. 568)
4. A (p. 569)
5. C (p. 574)
6. B (p. 580-581)
7. D (p. 581)
8. D (p. 587-588)
9. B (p. 589)
10. A (p. 592)

SHORT ANSWER

1. A person is not responsible for criminal conduct if at the time of such conduct as a result of mental disease of defect he lacks substantial capacity either to appreciate the criminality (wrongfulness) of his conduct or to confirm his conduct to the requirements of law. (p. 566)

2. May be committed for longer period than they would have been imprisoned otherwise. May have difficulty proving they are no longer insane or dangerous. (p. 566-567)

3. Insanity deal with person's condition at the time of the crime. Competency deals with condition at the time of trial. (p. 568)

4. That "being responsible" is a social judgment, not a personality characteristic. That even "different" people have the right to be treated like everyone else. (p. 569-570)

5. If they are mentally ill AND dangerous to themself or others (which may include being unable to take care of themself). (p. 572-573)

6. 1) right to least restrictive alternative for treatment, 2) right to receive treatment, 3) right to refuse treatment. (p. 576-581)

7. Ethical codes and guidelines, Committees to review ethics of proposed research. (p. 584)

8. Right to freely consent (or refuse) to participate in research after being informed of the procedure and any risks involved. (p. 585)

9. 1) Therapist judges client is dangerous, 2) Client introduces his/her sanity in a trial, 3) Client accuses therapist of malpractice, 4) Client is victim of child abuse (in some states), 5) Client initiated therapy to evade or plan a crime (in some states). (p. 588)

10. There is no clear answer to this. Perhaps brief aversive treatment could prevent long term disability or death. Careful consideration of ethical, legal, and psychological implications is needed. (p. 593-595)